M000158670

A FIRESIDE BOOK

PUBLISHED BY SIMON & SCHUSTER INC.

New York • London • Toronto • Sydney • Tokyo • Singapore

ANDREA CAGAN

Awakening the Healer Within

Fireside

Simon & Schuster Building
Rockefeller Center
1230 Avenue of the Americas
New York, New York 10020

Copyright © 1990 by Andrea Cagan

All rights reserved
including the right of reproduction
in whole or in part in any form.

FIRESIDE and colophon are registered trademarks
of Simon & Schuster Inc.

Designed by Mary Sarah Quinn
Manufactured in the United States of America

10 9 8 7 6 5 4 3 2 1

Library of Congress Cataloging in Publication Data

Cagan, Andrea.
    Awakening the healer within / Andrea Cagan.
        p.   cm.
    "A Fireside book."
        1. Psychic surgery—Philippines.   2. Healers—Philippines.
3. Spiritual healing—Philippines.   I. Title.
RZ403.P75C34   1990   89-29551
615.8'52—dc20   CIP
ISBN 0-671-70087-1

Acknowledgments

I would like to thank Teri Kaufman for helping me to clean up and sort out my thoughts and ideas so that I could feel good about initially presenting this book. Thanks to Chris Griscom for being so available and opening the door for me.

I thank Shari Wenk for respecting and believing in me and Barbara Gess for choosing me and for her positive encouragement and wise suggestions.

I am grateful to Phil Heithaus, my photographer and friend, for going above and beyond the call of duty. I thank Katrina Raphaell for her friendship and tender guidance. And thanks to Stephanie Abbott for listening and reminding me Who was really running things when the going got tough.

I acknowledge all of the Philippine healers for being their amazing and loving selves, and especially the Reverend Alex Orbito for his cooperation, his mastery, and his loving friendship. I thank Jimmy Licauco for recognizing me, for all the laughs, and for being the most skeptical believer I have ever met.

I offer admiration and appreciation to my parents and my

sister, Jill, who pushed through their fears and preconceived ideas to become a loving support system.

Special thanks goes to my good friend Juliet Green, who guided me with love and expertise through every phase of the development of this project, extending herself as much as possible all along the way.

And my deepest gratitude goes to dearest Kevin for his constant love, strong support and wisdom, his sense of humor, and his warm right shoulder.

Andrea Cagan

TO "SEESTER LOOEE,"
MY SPIRITUAL TEACHER AND MY INSPIRATION,
I DEDICATE THIS BOOK,
FOR HER WISDOM, HER FRIENDSHIP, HER LAUGHTER,
HER LOVE,
AND HER ETERNAL YOUTH.

Author's Note

The account that follows was the result of three separate trips to the Philippines spanning the years 1982 to 1985. For the purposes of brevity and continuity, I have consolidated the time and left out the spaces in between. All the experiences and people presented are true. Whenever a name has been changed to protect privacy, it is indicated by a footnote.

Contents

Please note that *Awakening the Healer Within* reflects the personal experience of the author. The book is not to be interpreted as an endorsement of or a guide to psychic surgery or to any other form of self-healing. Psychic surgery is *not* a substitute for medical treatment. Any treatment from or consultation with psychic surgeons or other such healers must be undertaken at the patient's own risk.

Introduction

In the summer of 1982, I embarked upon a journey that changed my way of being in this world. I was invited to Manila by my dear friend and mentor, Dr. Lois Black-Hill, to observe the work of the Philippine psychic surgeons. I had heard tales of their abilities to painlessly penetrate the flesh with their bare hands and remove illness, leaving no scar. I considered it a fantasy until Lois showed me actual photographs of these operations. My journey, which began as a challenge to verify what I considered to be an impossible phenomenon, turned out to be a pathway to deep revelations within myself and my universe.

As children, many of us naturally possess certain psychic abilities. But like a muscle that atrophies from neglect, these gifts usually diminish and eventually disappear due to lack of personal and cultural support. Here in the West, psychic expression is not only frequently unrecognized, it is often met with antagonism and ridicule.

Conversely, in the Philippine culture, people are encouraged to embrace the extraordinary without question. As a result, psychic powers thrive and mature in an environment fertile with inspiration and profound faith. Those who exhibit paranormal powers are recognized, respected, and even protected so that their sensitivities may develop further, providing hope and much-needed service to a greatly expanding poverty-stricken nation.

From the moment that I saw flesh penetrated with bare hands, I found myself confronting a lifetime of rigid belief systems. I moved around in a state of shock, confused and filled with doubt and fear. What eventually enabled me to humbly accept the unacceptable was my experience of the immense degree of love and simplicity that the Philippine healers express in every aspect of their lives.

Unfortunately, the phenomenal act of penetrating the flesh has attracted more attention and notoriety than the question of whether or not the patient actually is healed. Due to our Western minds, it is logical that the investigation into this mystery must come first. But when we are dealing with realities that defy ordinary logic, the fact is that concrete proof is impossible. We can only attempt to lift the veils for ourselves as individuals by direct experience. During the course of my research, I have firmly established for myself that the healers can and actually do penetrate the flesh when need be. I have observed that they go into the body about forty percent of the time. For the other sixty percent, they use their abilities to magnetize and materialize diseased tissue on the surface of the patient's skin.

The Philippine healers feel that disease is lodged in the rigid belief systems of the mind. When a patient watches someone pass hands through the flesh, the belief systems are cracked open and the disease loses power as it is severed from its matrix. Sometimes healing can be accomplished without physical penetration, but as long as the more dramatic demonstration of psychic surgery is necessary for the patient's mind, the healers will continue to do it.

In my travels, I have come across charlatans who try to emulate the healers, either in an attempt to make money or to preserve their antiquated belief that such paranormal healing experiences are impossible. They stuff chicken parts up their sleeves and do sleight-of-hand to manipulate others. These frightened and misguided individuals create tragic consequences, often robbing people of their final hope for survival. In many walks of life there exists a vast number of insecure people who try to make their living by feeding off the extraordinary deeds of others. In light of this fact, it becomes necessary for us to increase our awareness, so that we may discern the difference for ourselves between fakery and truth.

For myself, I found that the intellectual rewards for deepening my research into this mind-boggling reality were more unanswerable and frustrating questions. I have come to realize that the only way to have peace of mind while exploring the mysteries of life is to forget about trying to figure them out intellectually and simply accept and rejoice in the fact that, if there are indeed mysteries, they will by definition remain mysterious and will never be totally understood. Once this attitude is reached, the more important question has an opportunity to surface: Does anybody get healed?

With psychic surgery, success ultimately has more to do with the patient than the healer. I have seen two people with identical problems and identical treatments come away with completely different results. The ones with the positive attitudes, who believe that they are responsible for their own healing, have a far greater chance to heal than those who feel helpless and look to others to take them out of their victimized circumstances. It is participating with receptivity and complete cooperation, patient with healer, that will allow the greatest chance for success.

I was never interested in compiling data or case histories on patients because my involvement came from a spiritual calling. I have, however, seen reports that were corroborated by the healers themselves that among their medically diagnosed terminally ill patients, they have about a twenty percent success rate of complete recovery. For less serious ailments, the percentage rises.

As a researcher, I feel it is not my responsibility to try to convince anyone of the validity of psychic surgery. People must find the truth for themselves. But I have acquired a wealth of experience in this field, and for those who are ready, I feel inspired to let them know that true psychic healing really does exist.

In the many articles and documentaries I have seen about Philippine faith healing, the topic has been shrouded in illusion and presented in terms that are both confusing and misleading. It is my intention to dispel these illusions and to clearly report what I have personally observed and learned. I would not ask anyone to believe or disbelieve what I am reporting. I simply ask the reader to keep an open mind and accept that there are happenings that go beyond the logical, scientifically constructed ideas on which our beliefs are formed. It is only through the willingness to stay open to the possible existence of realities that we cannot yet explain that we progress and evolve.

It is my sincere wish that others may use my experience as inspiration and support to go wherever their hearts may lead. When we are able to dissolve the separation between ourselves and our visions, we create an opening to tap into and express the vast reservoir of greatness that exists within each one of us.

1

THE
CALLING

The wooden heels of my Dr. Scholl's step-in shoes made a loud clopping sound as I ran down the stairs leading into the underground spa. Rounding the corner, the first thing I saw was the receptionist, looking up to see who was disturbing the tranquillity of this healing environment.

I controlled my breath, lightened my step and in a quiet voice let her know that I had come to see what types of treatments were available. She handed me a schedule and, without a word, motioned to me to take a seat. Obediently, I sat and began to consider each of the delicious-sounding possibilities: Swedish massage, Shiatsu, salt rubs, hot oil scalp treatments, and aloe vera facials. I touched the skin on my cheeks, and decided that what I really needed was a facial. It seemed that my skin had greatly suffered from the crazy life-style I had been leading for the last several years.

I stepped back over to the receptionist and stood in front of her for a few moments before she looked up from the book on acupuncture she was reading. She looked at me questioningly and I wondered if she was able to speak.

"I'd like to sign up for a facial, please," I told her.

"Fine. We have an opening with Lois at three-thirty," she whispered. "Name and room number, please."

"Andrea Cagan. Room number seven," I whispered back.

She took down the information, picked up her book and returned to her silence, completely ignoring me. I stood for a moment, staring down at my feet, then at the walls around me, unsure what to do next. Since I had two hours before my treatment, I headed back upstairs, trying to quiet my shoes by gripping with my toes. Once outside, I returned to my normal speedy pace, ran over to the pools and slid into the hot mineral water that has made this desert resort famous.

The heat of the water and the healing essence of the minerals soaked into my body, reminding me how stressed I felt. The tension began to slowly break up like clouds of thick brown smog being washed away by a downpour. Through this heaviness I saw flashes of the last two years of my life and the people I had been spending my time with.

Like so many others, I had left New York City for California in pursuit of an acting career. I had been a professional ballet dancer since I was sixteen, but I had become disenchanted. I decided to go for a dream and try my luck in Hollywood. Things had started out well for me. Now I was doing some national TV commercials but aside from the money, I had no real interest in the work. Leaving the highly disciplined routine of the ballet had been confusing, and Hollywood had really gotten to me. Too many parties, too many drugs, not enough real people and not enough good reasons to get up in the morning.

I had gone through a short "spiritual" phase, which included reading a few books on positive thinking and trying my hand at some yoga and meditation with crystals. This relaxed me a little bit, but I dropped it quickly because I was too disconnected from myself to gain any substantial results.

I was basically uninspired. My life had changed from one

of discipline and good health to late-night parties and lots of cocaine. I spent most of my time figuring out how to escape reality.

I had learned about this resort from Laurie, my closest friend for eleven years. We had become inseparable after a film we had done together in 1971. But over the last few years, although the bond was still strong, we hadn't seen as much of each other. I had become involved in a destructive life-style that she wasn't interested in being a part of. When she had described the mineral waters and the wonderful treatments this place offered, I had called immediately to make a reservation, knowing how much I craved the peaceful surroundings, a place to be alone and think.

While my body luxuriously soaked in the healing minerals, I gratefully lost my mind in the puffy cloud formations that reminded me of simpler days. It had been a long time since I had really relaxed. I envied the ease with which the cloud shapes took form and then dissolved into something else in their ever-changing motion. Wondering if my life would ever change back into something that I could be proud of, I fought the demons and rode the huge creatures in the sky until a few minutes before 3:30.

Facing a sign that said PRIVATE, I lightly knocked on the door to Lois's facial room. The penetrating aroma of desert sage trickled out as the door opened to reveal a small middle-aged blond woman with a smile that seemed to reach much further than the corners of her mouth. I stepped inside the dimly lit room and, although I was standing in a wet bathing suit, I wasn't the slightest bit cold. It was as if Lois's warmth had seeped into every corner.

"Hi, I'm Lois," she said in a loud whisper. She motioned to another door at the other side of the room that opened into the spa. She rolled her eyes as if to let me know that whispering was not her favorite mode of communication but necessary in these circumstances.

"You can take off your suit and lie down on the massage table. I'll be right back." Lois left the room while I disrobed and covered myself with the sheet that was provided.

I lay down on my back and examined the nearest wall. It was covered with autographed photos of the friends and movie stars who were Lois's clients. The door opened and Lois came in holding some fresh towels. She took a seat behind me, turned on a strong magnifying lamp and, placing it several inches above my face, began to study the pores of my skin.

"Well, you really need a facial," she understated kindly. "It looks like the right time to start a good skin-care program."

With fingers that felt like feathers, she gently began to wash my face with her healing creams, as I spilled out my life to her. I told her about leaving the ballet, about my bad marriage and divorce, my frustrations with my career; I even told her about the drugs. I talked until there was nothing left to tell and she just listened silently, systematically cleaning my skin.

It seemed that Lois's hands were not only touching the outside surface of my face. They were also reaching inside my head and caressing the negativity away, transforming what felt like masses of blocked energy into clear, sparkling light. I opened my eyes for a moment. Lois's face seemed to have become so large, was taking up so much space, that there was no room for my senseless mind chatter. I was compelled to relax.

When she had finished cleaning my skin, she covered my face with a cool herbal mask.

"You are no longer a thirty-year-old woman. I want you to see yourself as a child," she crooned. "You are running free in the most beautiful place that you can imagine. Your skin is perfect, youthful, and radiant. And so are you."

Light strains of ethereal music began to fill the air while Lois gently touched my hands and feet, sending tingling sensations through my arms and legs. I lost my physical orientation, having no idea which side of the room I was facing. Then I was no longer in the room at all. I was in another place that looked like the operating room of a hospital. Lois was with me and we were wearing white gowns. I was holding the hands and she the feet of a man lying on a table, obviously prepared to undergo surgery. I was in a deep state of concentration, allowing a strong flow of energy to pass through the top of my head and out my hands into the hands of the patient. I could see him begin to relax as we soothed him into a peaceful state of unconsciousness. We must have been administering some sort of psychic anesthesia.

When my awareness returned to the present, I was lying on the massage table, the dried, hardened mask making my face pulsate. I heard the soft sound of Lois's footsteps as she returned to the room. I had not heard her leave. She covered my face with a warm wet towel which softened the hard herbal mixture. In a few more minutes, Lois removed it with a towel and my skin was tingling. She massaged every part of my face until all the tension was gone. Then she struck a match and lit a piece of dried sage. Holding this leaf several inches above my skin, she traced the outline of my entire body, blessing me and allowing the last vestiges of stress to burn up in the sweet-smelling smoke. I was brand new.

Lois flipped on the light and looked at me. "Your face looks great! What a glow!" she said. "Take a look." She pointed toward a mirror on the wall. As I admired my new face, photographs that had been tacked up just below the mirror caught my eye. It was a series of three pictures of a man standing over a woman who was lying on a table. I was horrified to discover that his fingers were buried to the first knuckle inside her abdomen and there was blood surrounding his hands and on her stomach. My first impulse was to turn away, but the realization that Lois was the woman on the table made me look closer.

"What is this?" I asked her.

"Oh, that is what they call 'psychic surgery' in the Philippines. Have you ever heard of it?" she asked.

"What is he doing to you?" I demanded, completely ignoring her question.

"He's removing a cyst from my stomach," she answered, quite matter-of-factly.

"Doesn't it hurt?"

"Not at all. Look at my face."

Her face in the photograph was totally relaxed. In fact, she was actually looking at the camera and smiling.

"How does he do that?" I asked.

"It's a spiritual gift that some of the Filipinos have. They call it bare-handed surgery. They're able to penetrate the flesh with their bare hands, without instruments, and remove illness. When they're finished, they withdraw their hands and there is no scar."

In answer to the incredulous look on my face, Lois unbuttoned her pants on the spot and pulled them partway down, revealing the bare skin on her abdomen. It was unblemished.

Lois pulled out a scrapbook and we spent the next twenty minutes paging through numerous photographs of her various Philippine trips over the last several years. I bought some of her skin-care products, promising myself that I would actually use them. For the first time in a couple of years, I had the sense that I wanted to start caring for myself again. Throughout the rest of the day, I could feel Lois's presence all around me. I saw her magnetic smile, felt her caring hands touching my face. I forgot to get high that night and slept a deep, dreamless sleep. I drove back home to Los Angeles the next morning, knowing that something had shifted.

During the next few weeks, I tried to settle back into the old routine, but a new sense of boredom had set in. Auditions for commercials and films that I cared nothing about filled my days. The evenings were spent with acquaintances, mostly getting high, sitting around and talking about the things that we wished we were doing. I found that I was going home earlier than usual and eventually, I started staying home. The life I was living became less and less interesting to me. My extreme loneliness became almost unbearable, and I could sense Lois around me a great deal of the time. At night, before I dropped off to sleep, I would often see flashes of the photographs of the Philippine healers. I didn't understand how such a thing as barehanded surgery could be possible, but I couldn't get it off my mind. It was as if I were being haunted.

One Saturday morning I got up, packed a bag and got into my car. I was going back to the desert. I was tired of the self-destructive life I was living. I was tired of making money by selling products on TV that I didn't believe in and would never dream of using. I wanted something better for myself and somehow, Lois was a key.

I stood in front of the PRIVATE sign, my heart pounding so loudly I was certain I didn't have to knock. The door opened, and as I entered the room I was relieved to find that it was still all there: the sweet smells, the compelling photos on the wall, and Lois. We hugged warmly and, after offering me a seat at her desk, Lois jumped up onto the massage table. She sat facing me, looking like a playful child with her mischievous smile and her feet dangling several inches above the floor.

"Your skin looks wonderful. You have that glow!" she complimented me.

I looked into her eyes and I knew what I wanted to say. "It doesn't work anymore. I can't keep going on in the same way. I kept seeing your face and I don't know what to do. I need some help."

She stood up.

"Come on. Let's take a walk."

Lois took an enormous straw sun hat off a rack in the corner and placed it on her head. I could hardly see her face anymore. I followed her outside. We walked in silence for a short while, merging with the heat and stillness of the desert. As I turned sideways to talk to her, I was surprised to find myself staring down at the top of her sun hat. She had such a huge presence that I hadn't noticed she was actually several inches shorter than I. For the second time, I began to speak to her about things I had never expressed to anyone else.

I told her about how disoriented I had been since I left the ballet. I explained how different everything had seemed after I had met her. I told her about my vision during the facial, in which she and I had ministered to a patient, and about the impact the photographs had had on me. I described how I would see them each night before I went to sleep. I needed to know what to do next. I asked her for guidance. She listened quietly before speaking.

"You have to look inside and find out what's right for you. Nobody can tell you that. But you don't have to stay stuck in anything that doesn't feel good. I've started over again many times and it always turned out better than the time before. You have the power to change whatever you want. It's all at your fingertips."

We stopped walking and turned to face each other.

"I want to go to the Philippines with you," I blurted out.

Lois's face burst out into a huge smile.

"I know the feeling," she said. "It was in 1976 that I first heard about the Philippine healers. I was a journalist for a newspaper at the time and I was so intrigued that I asked for an assignment to go over there and do a story on them. My request was granted and that was the beginning."

She invited me over to her little desert house where she prepared a special dinner of Ukrainian food like her mother used to make. We sat up talking late into the night, discussing our future trip. Dr. Lois Black-Hill, being a doctor of naturopathy,* was already familiar with the world of alternative healing before she met the Philippine healers. She told me how quickly they had accepted her into their world. She now considered them to be her dearest friends and she went back each year to

---

*A system of treating illness that avoids drugs and uses natural agents such as air, water, and organic herbs.

see them and study with them. Lois already had plans to return in the early part of July. That was only a month away. She seemed to be willing to take me along and there was no question in my mind that I wanted to go with her. I really had nothing to lose, nothing of any true value to leave behind. After meeting with her only twice, I trusted Lois implicitly and I somehow knew that as long as I stuck with her, I had nothing to worry about.

I spent the night at her house and left for home early the next day. I had a lot to do. I had to renew my passport, call my agents, break the news to my parents and arrange for someone to stay in my apartment. I was leaving for Manila in thirty days.

2

ARRIVAL

I was never so glad to get off a plane in my life. After seventeen hours of traveling, my clothes were stuck to my body and my legs felt heavy and clumsy. I instantly broke out into a sweat as the humid air engulfed me. Lois and I stumbled into a chaotic mess of yelling people, immigration agents, and totally disorganized baggage claim rituals. Manila airport was complete pandemonium.

The walls in the terminal were gray and peeling, the obvious result of perpetual exposure to very high humidity. I piled my hair on top of my head to wipe off the perspiration running down the back of my neck. Cigarette smoke choked me. Wherever I looked, olive-brown faces with slanted eyes stared back at me, and it occurred to me that I was the one who was different. Squeaky conveyor belts loudly announced the arrival of our luggage and we had to fight to keep our position among the crowds of people in order to spot our bags. We finally extricated our suitcases from behind the multitudes of tied-up, overstuffed cardboard boxes which Lois jokingly called "Philippine luggage."

We were quickly waved through customs and as we proceeded out the front door five different men rushed us, fighting each other to lead us to their taxis. Amid the confusing mass of people and the cacophony of sound, we suddenly heard a loud, commanding voice shout. The taxi drivers parted and there stood our warrioress in shining armor, Chuchi de Vega.

"Lois, Lois!" she yelled. She shoved several people out of her way and hugged Lois hard. Chuchi's well-trained driver grabbed our bags, threw them into her black Mercedes and motioned for us to get in. We didn't hesitate for an instant. Lois told the driver, "Manila Midtown Hotel," and we were off in a flash.

Lois had met Chuchi during one of her previous trips to the Philippines. Chuchi was a short, feisty woman with tremendous energy. Her husband had held a very powerful position in the Philippine government until he was assassinated in the mid-seventies. Chuchi was left alone to single-handedly raise her three children, which she had done with great success. Over the years she had accumulated some important tools: a voice that could shatter glass and a tremendous sense of humor. She chattered in perfect English about the difficult political situation under the dictator Ferdinand Marcos, how her children were doing in school, and the intensely humid weather that was driving everyone crazy. She seemed in total command of herself and I liked her immediately.

As we drove through the streets, there was heavily congested traffic, even at this early hour of six in the morning. Private cars, taxis, and jeepneys (the local mode of public transportation) were spewing black diesel fumes from their tail pipes. It seemed that the entire city was already awake and moving. I opened the window to get a better look at the small bonfires by the sides of the road. A stream of hot air hit me in the face and my nose was instantly filled with the charred smell of burning wood.

I had a déjà vu. The smell played inside my nostrils like a reminder of a lost world that had come back to haunt me.

"They are burning coconut palm fronds to make fires to cook breakfast," Chuchi informed me.

We navigated through the crowded streets of Manila, turning down alleys that seemed to lead nowhere, and eventually we arrived at our hotel. Chuchi dropped us off and Lois promised that after we had rested, she would call and they could spend some time together.

The car door banged shut but we could still hear Chuchi yelling directions to the driver. We looked at each other and laughed out loud.

"That was Chuchi!" Lois said, shaking her head. "Let's check in, eat some decent food, and take a rest."

After we checked in, the bellboy led us up to the twelfth floor, to a small but comfortable room overlooking Manila Bay. We showered, unpacked, and fell onto the beds. We were exhausted from the trip and decided to order room service and try to go to sleep early.

But when I lay down to rest, sleep wouldn't come. My time clock was confused and although my body felt spent, my mind was wired and active. I began to review all that I had done during the last month to prepare for the trip, both physically and emotionally. I thought about my friend who was staying in my apartment back home, and hoped that he would pay the rent on time. I remembered how difficult it had been to decide what I would need in a place that was totally unknown to me. I mentally checked the drawers, hoping that I had brought the right clothes. I could feel my parents and my sister worrying about my well-being. I remembered their frightened reactions when I told them I was going to the Philippines on what seemed to them to be a whim. And now their fears had become my fears, and I wondered what in the world I was doing here.

A great deal of it had to do with Lois. She had touched a place inside of me that wanted to leave the self-destructive course I had been on. For the first time in several years, I wanted to take care of myself and feel good. I needed this time with her to reinforce that. But there was more.

My life had been stuck in such a rigid pattern of discomfort, it needed something completely alien to my normal existence to pull me out. The photographs of the healers had represented that hope. They were like a seductive whisper in my ear, so compelling that it couldn't be ignored. I was ready to make a change and I had recognized this opportunity as a way out. My thoughts turned to Lois; I was so thankful that we had met. I heard her roll over in her bed and wondered if she was also having trouble sleeping.

"Are you awake?" I whispered.

"Yes. I can't sleep. Let's put on the light."

We sat up in bed and grinned at each other.

"It's a sixteen-hour time difference and it feels like the middle of the morning," she said. "It takes a little time to adjust."

She turned to face me with her eyes glowing.

"Do you remember the man you saw in the photographs? He is the Reverend Alex Orbito, one of the most powerful healers in the Philippines. I was lucky enough to meet him the first time I came here. I was very impressed not only by his work but also by his willingness to mix with his patients and onlookers. When I returned the next year, he remembered me and greeted me warmly. He allowed me to stand close to him while he worked and to take as many photographs as I wished. Last year, Alex granted me a private interview about his life. Since you're going to meet him tomorrow morning, perhaps you'd like to hear about him." And she proceeded to tell me his story.

"Alex was born on November 25, 1940, in a small town about 100 miles northwest of Manila," Lois began. "He was the youngest of fourteen children, his parents being very poor farmers who tilled the land for others. Both his mother and father were very spiritually adept people and were among the founders of the early Spiritualist movement. Of the six surviving children, four of them became healers. But Alex is the best known and supposedly the most gifted.

"According to him, he led a rather normal childhood," Lois continued, "except for certain dreams and visions which often came to him in the form of a wise old man with white hair and a long beard. Alex now interprets these visions as the appearance of his spirit guide, who came to guide him to his healing work.

"He said that one night, when he was fourteen years old, he had a dream that he healed an old woman who had been crippled for many years. In the dream, after laying hands on her, he watched her get up out of her wheelchair and walk. As soon as he awoke in the morning, there was a knock on the door. It was a young boy who had been sent by his crippled mother to fetch Alex. He went with the boy and when he appeared at the door, there was the old woman from his dream.

"He spent twenty minutes with her, praying and rubbing coconut oil on her crippled legs. Then he stopped praying, stepped back, and said, 'You get up, now.' For the first time in ten years, the woman stood up, and without hesitation began to walk around the room. Can you imagine how Alex must have felt? Needless to say, the word spread quickly that young Orbito was a powerful healer."

I moved closer to Lois, propping myself up on my elbows. A completely captive audience, I felt like a child listening to a fantastic fairy tale.

"Alex says that each day, when he arrived home from school, there were people lined up at his door, waiting for healing. Being only fourteen, it was more than he could handle, so he made secret plans to leave home. He told no one of his scheme, not even his closest friends, and one day he fled and took up residence in a province several days journey from his real home. He changed his name to Joseph Viloria, rented a small room, and got a job assisting a photographer. Learning photography was satisfying to him and he relished his freedom and privacy. But it didn't last long.

"Early one morning, after being at a party all night, he arrived at the studio before anyone else. He lay down to nap, only to be rudely awakened by a hard slap on the face. It was the police. They handcuffed him and dragged him to jail. After they had thrown him in a cell, he was informed that his employer's photographic equipment had been stolen and they were sure that Alex was the culprit.

"He sat in jail for days, not knowing what to do and praying that the real thief would be found. One night, he heard voices speaking to him. They promised to help him if he would agree to go back home and use the healing gifts he had been given. He did not know what to make of this but he agreed, if only he could be let out of this terrible place. The next morning he was set free, for they had found the real thief."

I let out my breath in a huge sigh of relief. Lois looked at me, amused, and went on.

"But after Alex was released, he was still reluctant to live the life of a healer. He knew that he could never really make money, that people would be hounding him and he would never be able to do what he wanted. Can you understand why he could not bring himself to return? He wandered to the next town and rented a room in which to contemplate his predicament. He did not have long to think because he became seriously ill. He lay in bed, burning up with a very high fever, and once again he heard the voices saying, 'Why have you abandoned us? Go home and keep your word or you will die in this place.'

"He knew that this was his last chance and somehow he got himself to the bus station and headed for home. The closer he got, the better he felt, until by the time he arrived at his home province, the fever had completely disappeared. The illness, however, had left him very weak and he could hardly walk. His parents cared for him for three months until he was completely recovered.

"He then began his healing practice full time but did not receive the power to do the actual bare-handed operations until several years later. Now he is tremendously dedicated to his healing work, but he has always retained his interest in other things. So he opened Orbit Tours and Travel Agency. The name is rather appropriate, don't you think?"

I nodded in agreement.

"Alex's travel agency is in this hotel. We'll go there first thing in the morning," she said.

I yawned, realizing that I was getting very sleepy.

Lois smiled at me. "I'm tired now, too. Let's see if we can sleep. Tomorrow, the real adventure begins."

3

FIRST
EXPOSURE

I awakened in the morning to find Lois's bed empty. She had told me she would be going down early to meet Alex, but I was surprised that I had not heard her get up. There was even a breakfast tray on the table by the window. I was usually a very light sleeper but the time change must have affected me more than I realized. Feeling rather disoriented, I showered and dressed. I munched a bite of sweet, juicy papaya, took a few sips of very strong coffee, and headed downstairs after Lois.

The elevator door opened with a loud grinding sound to reveal the lobby of the Manila Midtown Hotel. I stepped out into a busy, colorful scene, with people from every imaginable nationality acting out a Monday morning. I passed by women in suits, men in traditional Philippine Barong Tagalog business shirts, and children being dragged along by their mothers so that they wouldn't get lost. An Indian woman with an exotic red dot painted on her forehead walked alongside her husband, his head meticulously wrapped in a white cotton covering. Bellboys brushed past me, pushing overfilled carts of luggage to the elevator area. Not exactly sure which way to go, I headed down the hallway of the lobby, following an arrow that pointed toward SHOPS AND BUSINESSES.

I walked by novelty shops selling multicolored shells, pearl jewelry, and native hand-woven clothing, but I merely glanced in as I passed, eager to reach my destination. Situated at the end of the hall were two adjacent travel agencies. I quickened my pace, stopping at the farthest one. At the top of the glass windows was a conspicuous, brightly painted neon sign reading ORBIT TOURS AND TRAVEL. I knew I had arrived.

Lois ushered me in and introduced me to four smiling people behind desks. They were Alex's employees and were very gracious and pleased to meet me. I noticed several other people: a family of three, and a couple, apparently waiting for something. Lois pulled up an empty chair for me and I sat beside her while she informed me that Alex was already here and doing healing in the back room of the travel agency.

A woman's head appeared from behind a brown door and looked at Lois.

"Reverend Orbito will see you now," she informed us in a high sing-songy voice.

Lois turned to me and whispered, "You're going to see it and you're still not going to believe it. Come on." And she led me through the little entranceway, closing both the door and the world as I once knew it behind us.

The inner office was quite dark and small, hardly more than a cubicle, and any available space was filled with strange furniture. There was a slightly torn leather couch and a massage table covered with a sheet showing what looked like light traces of bloodstains. A Bible, a dish of wet cotton balls, and an empty bowl rested on the table. Wedged into the back corner, seated behind an oversized desk, sat a very thin Asian man, dressed in a suit and tie, smoking a cigarette. I knew immediately that it had to be Alex because in this dimly lit room, a glow radiated around him as if there were a skylight above his head. When he spotted us, he broke into a huge smile, his shining white teeth contrasting against his extremely dark skin; he rose to greet us. He hugged Lois for a long time, obviously delighted to see her, and then he turned his gaze to me.

As his eyes met mine, I was flooded with warmth, similar to the feeling I had when I first met Lois. He gently reached out to shake my hand, and although his fingers felt soft and almost insubstantial, they sent pulses of energy traveling up my arm. He motioned for us to sit in a couple of imitation leather chairs, walked over to the woman who had let us in, and said something to her in their native language, Tagalog. She then left us alone. As he returned to his desk I studied him with great interest, because he seemed different from anyone I had ever met.

Alex was short, about five foot three in stocking feet, and he was extremely thin and small-boned. He wore high-heeled boots that made him walk quite awkwardly, and he had the tiniest waist I have ever seen on a man. When he sat, he was completely dwarfed by his desk. He offered us both a cigarette, which we declined, and as he fingered his gold engraved lighter I noticed his perfectly manicured fingernails and delicate, graceful hands. The wall behind him was covered with plaques of honor and humanitarian awards that had been bestowed upon him by many different organizations over the past twenty years. He was sporting a thin dark moustache, which he laughingly told us, in a very thick accent, was "imported from Germany." Apparently he had just returned and was decidedly glad to be back home.

He and Lois chatted for a few minutes and then she said, "Alex, do you feel like doing an operation? My neck is giving me a little trouble."

"Yah, okay," he answered. "You lie down."

In one second flat, Lois had whipped off her blouse and was lying face down on the massage table. Alex got up slowly, took off his jacket, and walked over to Lois. He paused by the side of the table, picked up the Bible and lowered his head in prayer for several minutes. Then he looked at me and indicated that I might come closer if I so wished. I went to stand beside him. He placed his hands gently on the top vertebra of Lois's neck and began to move his fingers around to locate the exact trouble spot. Apparently he found it, for in the next minute, he closed his eyes, made a slight grimace, and I heard a sharp popping sound while the fingers of his left hand disappeared up to the first knuckle, inside Lois's back.

It didn't matter that I had seen the photographs. It didn't matter that Lois had given me her descriptions and explanations. Nothing could have prepared me for this moment. I was too surprised to gasp. My body broke out in chills. I quickly looked over at Lois's face, afraid that she must be in terrible pain, but she appeared to be completely relaxed. A small trickle of blood came to the surface while Alex masterfully maneuvered his fingers around under the flesh on the left side of Lois's spine.

I do not recall what happened next because as my mind began to register that I was watching someone put his hands into Lois's body, it was as if my brain shut off. All I could hear was my freaked-out mind telling me that what I was seeing could not be real. But I do remember that in about ten seconds, he was holding a long, clear stringy substance between the fingers of his right hand.

"Calcium." He pronounced the word slowly, holding it out for me to take a closer look. Then he dropped the substance in the empty bowl and grabbed a towel to wipe his hands. I looked at the top of Lois's neck and all that remained to tell the story was a slight red mark that looked vaguely like a fingernail scratch. He offhandedly wiped the towel over her back to remove any traces of blood and affectionately gave her neck a light pat. "Okay!" he said.

Lois jumped up, obviously delighted, and manipulated her neck a little to check out the area.

"Oh, Alex, thank you. That feels so much better," she said.

Alex turned to face me. "How about you?" he asked innocently.

I heard myself answer, "Well, I guess you could check the same place on my neck. It's been bothering me for a long time."

He stared at the top of my spine as though he could see through me and then said, "Yah, okay."

I was truly terrified but I behaved in what I thought was a casual manner. I felt as if everything had shifted to slow motion as I carefully unbuttoned my blouse, neatly laid it down beside me and listened to my mother's voice telling me that I shouldn't let those healers touch me. I walked the treacherous two feet to arrive at the haunted massage table that was surely lurking in another dimension. Still disturbed by the loud voices that were jabbering in my head, I reluctantly sat and then slowly swung my legs up on the table, turning over to lie down on my stomach. Alex moved close to me and quietly advised in my ear, "You pray."

It had been a long time since I had really prayed, but it's something you never forget, especially when you need it, so pray I did. Then he lightly tapped my head and I completely let go. It was not a conscious decision on my part—the moment he touched me, I felt instantly transported into an altered state of mind, one in which I had no fear and no considerations. And I knew that I could trust him.

I heard him whisper, "Relax," as his hands began to wiggle around on my back, searching for the exact spot. For the next few minutes, I was aware that his hands were touching me but I couldn't tell what he was doing. I could feel only a light scratching sensation, as if he had inadvertently nicked me with his fingernail.

It was only a few seconds before Lois said excitedly, "Andrea, look!" I raised my head and saw that Alex was dangling a piece of long, stringy stuff between his fingers. For a moment, I wondered what he was holding and why he was showing it to me and then I realized that that stuff had come out of my back. I felt the towel whisk across my back and I sat up quickly to look questioningly at Lois. I was overcome by a lightheaded sensation. Long prickly shots of energy began at the top of my spine and rapidly traveled down and through my left arm. Moving my arm around to stretch my neck and my head, I noticed that there was a new feeling in my spine and shoulder. It was freedom from a pain that I had long ago lost awareness of. Now that it was gone, I realized how much it had limited my movement.

I looked into Alex's eyes and said, "Thank you," and got up from the massage table. He nodded his head and did the high-heeled hobble back to his chair, sat down, and lit up a cigarette.

"You rest now. You have jet lag. You come to my center tomorrow morning for the healing session. Nine o'clock, okay?"

We happily agreed to be there, thanked him again and exited out the door into the other world.

I spent the rest of the day in a daze of excitement and awe. I was not quite sure what I had experienced, because it had all happened so quickly, but I was definitely aware of what I was feeling. The energy pulses that were traveling through my body did not slow down. In fact, they accelerated and I spent most of the afternoon lying in bed with my eyes closed, tuning in to these amazing new sensations. I wanted to nap but I could not because I was too wired. My mind was working overtime making up excuses and logical explanations for what I had just seen. But the feelings in my body kept reminding me that something extraordinary had truly happened. Lois briefly explained to me that it was important to rest and keep water away from the area so that nothing would interfere with the healing process. Water could wash away the positive healing energy. She also told me that the electromagnetic energy that the healer uses to perform the surgery would travel through my body for up to twenty-four hours afterward, allowing the healing process to continue. I accepted what she said without question because, at this point, I was not really looking for answers. My brain was already holding more information than it knew what to do with. While

I tried, with great difficulty, to translate into understandable terms what I had just been through, I felt that answers could prove unsettling, because I was not yet sure how much of this truth I was willing to accept.

Here I was in the Philippines, exposing myself to a reality that was challenging the basic physical laws that I knew to be true. Why hadn't I just stayed home and found a new direction in a world that was familiar to me? What was it within me that had called me here to explore this particular territory? Why was I letting my mind be totally turned inside out? If I came to accept what had happened as true, what would that do to my life? Was it already too late to blend back into my old existence? I allowed these questions to lightly float through my consciousness like a swan drifting lazily across a reflecting lake on a summer day, with no immediate need to be noticed or attended to. I saw my reflection in the liquid pool of my third eye as I drifted downstream, and felt no more significant than one of my unanswered questions.

4

MELTING
BELIEFS

Beliefs are like clouds—
At first, they are strong and defined,
And it's so easy to see them,
Get safety from them.

Then, slowly and unmercifully,
The edges start a slow dissolve.
They change, they stretch and moan,
And remind us of other things.

They move and fade until
We can't see them anymore.
They are no longer valid
Because they no longer exist,

And did they ever exist?
Weren't they always something else, first?

My knuckles were beginning to hurt from clutching the handle in front of me as our taxi driver sped us through the crowded streets of Manila, masterfully dodging people and oncoming traffic. There are no lanes or traffic laws in this heavily congested city, and it appeared to be every man for himself. When the right side of the road was crowded, the driver would move with precision into the left, heading with breakneck speed straight toward the headlights of the oncoming cars. At the last possible moment, the car next to us would miraculously move over just enough to provide a minimum of space, and our driver, without applying the brakes, would neatly slide in.

The city was a staggering mass of color and sound, the streets filled with children on their way to school, merchants singing out their stories, and beggars crying their tales of woe. The traffic was dense and noisy, slowly honking and weaving its way through the town like a brightly colored caterpillar, pressing forward with every swerve of its creeping, massive body.

After about thirty minutes, our driver came to a screeching halt at Alex's house and deposited Lois, me, and my nervous stomachache in front of a bright orange wrought-iron door. He smiled broadly at our generous tip and wildly took off down the street, stalking his next victims.

It was with both anticipation and dread that I passed through this iron gateway, eager to see what came next and afraid of what I might find to further upset my equilibrium. I seemed to be maintaining a delicate inner balance, but I wasn't exactly sure how much I could take in and keep myself together.

Lois led me into a courtyard fronting a very large old wooden house. Beside the house were long rows of benches that looked like the pews of a church. In the courtyard, tall shade trees towered above several seated people who were eating hard-boiled eggs and freshly cooked sweet corn. When they saw Lois, a group of these people rushed to her, yelling out her name, and hugged her warmly. Several of them hugged me, too. They ushered us to seats on one of the benches. At the front of the group stood a preacher, leading a service in Tagalog. Although I could not understand him, I could feel his strong and persuasive energy. The perspiration was pouring down his face and he looked inspired and totally involved in what he was doing. After he noticed us, he smiled and mopped his brow. He addressed his congregation in heavily accented English.

"We have our friends here from America. They have come very far to see us so I will speak in English so that they may also receive the word of God."

Someone ran down the aisle and handed him an English Bible. Fortunately, most of the people could understand, English being their second language. With his hands on the Bible, he spoke to us of illness and healing, trying to make the people aware that a healer is not a magician or a saint. He is merely an instrument of God through which the energy of the Holy Spirit can pass. It is up to the patients to become aware of how they have taken on their illnesses, for without this awareness, an effective healing can never take place. He closed his eyes, murmured some words in Tagalog, and randomly opened the Bible. He blindly passed his hand over the page, intuitively stopping at a certain passage. Opening his eyes, he began to read aloud.

As I scanned the crowd to see how the people were responding, I caught sight of a small girl, squirming uncomfortably in her seat. She looked very bored. A slightly older boy sitting next to her began secretly to tickle her tummy and she was doing her best to control her desire to giggle. I had a strong urge to laugh while I watched them, remembering my days of sitting in the temple next to my father, and how he used to try to make me laugh. I could still recall that delicious feeling of containing my hysteria, knowing that I couldn't laugh out loud, certain that I would either burst open or wet my pants.

Behind the preacher was a small room enclosed by glass windows. A large picture of Jesus was on the wall, beside a gold banner with writing on it. Now I knew for sure I wasn't in temple. It read: UNION ESPIRITISTA CRISTIANA DE PILIPINAS (Christian Spiritist Union of the Philippines), REV. ALEX ORBITO, CORAZON DE AMOR DE ESPIRITU SANTO (Loving Heart of the Holy Spirit). This was obviously the healing room. I watched several women bring in bottles of oil, soak cotton balls in water, and wipe off the plastic cloth covering on the massage table. When he was finished, the preacher stepped down and the women came to get Lois and me, leading us through the mass of people toward the front of the room. We passed the kitchen to the main house on our way, and the pungent odor of fish, garlic, and frying fat jumped into my nose, nearly taking my breath away. Luckily, we kept walking and the women motioned for us to stand with them, just inside the healing room. I felt embarrassed to walk in, with all those people waiting outside, but the women were insistent that we remain with them. It seemed that foreigners were treated better than natives.

While I was still reeling from the pervasive odor of the Philippine cuisine, my attention became focused on a round and beautiful woman named Mary. She gently touched my arm with strong hands and then, with her loud, deep voice, she began to lead the entire group in a religious song. Lois whispered to me that they were singing an invocation to bring in the energy of the Holy Spirit to assist in the healing. It was good that they sang in Tagalog because all of this was very alien to my Jewish upbringing, and I was better off not understanding the words. I had never considered myself a religious person, and the crucifixes and references to Jesus were far from any frame of reference that I was accustomed to.

The sound of their songs was so touching and sweet that by the time they finished, not only were tears running down my cheeks, but I was actually singing along, even though I did not speak their language. Alex entered the room sometime during the third song; he sat on a chair behind the table, picked up his Bible, and prayed. I was fascinated by how different he looked from the day before. He was very serious, totally immersed in prayer and very deep within himself. I flashed back to the operations I had seen the day before. What wonders would he perform today?

He stood and made hand gestures from the Bible to the healing items on the table. If I squinted my eyes while I watched him, I could almost see a streak of light pass from the Bible to the table, while he transferred energy from one to the other. Lois informed me that this was his blessing and sterilization process. Once he infused his healing items with the energy of the Holy Spirit, all risk of infection was considered to be automatically eliminated. I hoped that she was right as I watched two of the largest black tropical water bugs that I had ever seen chase each other across the stone floor and come to rest under the healing table. It appeared that this was the romantic environment that they had chosen for their mating ritual. Suddenly, several large dogs that were tied up outside began to bark and howl, joining in the chorus of the last song. Their raspy voices were extremely loud and distracting, but Alex never batted an eyelash, completely focused on what he was doing.

The singing and howling ended and Alex sat back down, acknowledging our presence with a quick nod. His movements were constrained, with the obvious intention of conserving every bit of energy. He gracefully took a cotton ball between his fingers and waited, his hand poised tentatively at the edge of the table, his fingers alive with energy. While all of Alex's movements appeared to be in a silent slow motion, the women kicked into high gear, herding the chaotic crowds of people into the room, loudly calling out orders, and quickly and brusquely arranging everyone into two organized lines.

Mary let me stand beside her as she hustled the first patient onto the table. She quickly yanked the woman's skirt down beneath her navel and said to me, "Liver." Alex took a wet cotton ball in his hand, and, approaching the woman, he lightly placed his hands on her stomach. He hesitated for a moment with his eyes closed, locating the exact trouble area, and then he began to move his fingers. When they entered her flesh, the sound of a loud popping sent shivers through my body and I thought my brain had exploded. Blood escaped through Alex's fingers which Mary instantly wiped off with dry cotton. In one second more, his hand was wrist-deep inside the woman's stomach, apparently cleaning out the diseased tissue in her liver. His hands remained in her body for about twenty seconds while he squished them about, until I saw the fingers of his right hand emerge, grasping some very dark material that looked like old blood clots.

With his left hand remaining in her body, he removed the clots with his right hand, dropping them into the bowl that one of the other women had provided him. He reached back into the opening, and pulled out a smaller amount of the dark material, dropping it into the bowl. He then slowly and carefully removed his hands completely. The woman's stomach was covered with a light layer of blood which Mary cleaned off, a slight redness being the only remaining evidence that it had been open just a few moments before. While they were whisking the woman off the table, Alex dipped his hands into a bowl of water that one of his assistants had provided. I couldn't believe that this was his entire cleansing process between patients, but sure enough, he turned around and started working on the eyes of another person who was sitting in the chair beside him.

The session moved like an intricately choreographed dance, well-rehearsed and finely tuned, all performers carrying out their designated roles in perfect harmony. I watched operation after operation, seeing the same incredible thing each time, yet not believing what I was seeing. My stomachache had persisted, but I was too engrossed in watching the activity to consider doing anything about it. Alex continued his work, moving from table to chair to table with the ease and fluidity of a seasoned assembly-line worker.

Mary gave me one-word explanations for the various ailments of each patient. The illnesses ran the gamut from the minor troubles of sinus blockages and small cysts to tumors, hemorrhoids, cataracts, and terminal cancer. One patient sat in the chair and pointed to his nose. After rubbing his little finger in holy oil, Alex proceeded to stick it straight up the man's right nostril, nearly as far as his eye, his knuckle completely disappearing. After he withdrew his finger, he told the patient, "Sneeze!" The man blew hard and something that looked like a piece of hard, pink tissue flew out of his nose, bounced off Alex's chair, and landed at the other end of the table. Alex burst out laughing and said, "Like atomic bomb!" Mary took a quick moment out of her commanding position to join in the laughter and after reporting to me very matter-of-factly, "Polyp," she shoved someone back into his place in line.

More and more people kept appearing. After about forty-five minutes, Alex had easily worked on one hundred patients. I wondered how in the world he could keep going. He suddenly focused his eyes on my body, scanned me a moment and said, "Stomach. Please lie down."

Before I knew what hit me, Mary had hoisted me up on the table, unbuttoned my shorts, pulled them down past my waist, and was holding her cotton in readiness. Lois grabbed my camera and stood there in anticipation. I felt scared and uncomfortable, on display, as all the people gathered closer to watch. But as soon as Mary touched my head, a soothing energy began to infiltrate my body. Alex stood and prepared to work on me while the crowd of people fell away. He placed his hands on my stomach and closed his eyes. Although physically I remained where I lay, I felt as if I were being magically transported somewhere else. The quality of the light changed and everything looked softer and easier. I heard Alex say, "Relax," and the sound of the voices in the room became slightly muffled. Outside influences disappeared and I became aware of a gentle caress on my stomach. I lifted my head to see what Alex was doing and to my total amazement, I saw his hands immersed to the wrist in my stomach. Although my mind told me that this should be bothering me, I wasn't the slightest bit troubled or concerned. There was no pain at all and I remained with my head lifted off the table, calmly watching Alex moving his hands around in my stomach.

Mary turned to Lois and reported, "Acid," as if she were giving a computer readout. For me, it was all happening in slow motion and the chatter of people talking became nothing more than vague, indistinguishable sound. I was acutely aware of small details, tuned in to the constant clicking of the shutter of my camera as Lois busily snapped pictures. Strange, irrelevant thoughts passed through my mind about whether the film was slides or prints and where in this foreign land we could get it developed.

Just before he turned to wipe his hands, Alex looked straight into my eyes and I knew that he was not alone. I saw an intensity in his stare that did not belong only to him. It was as if someone or something else were looking out from behind his eyes. For a brief moment, we were locked in a stare that was not of this world and I knew that it was perfectly safe to trust this man. I also knew that I had been touched by a magical energy that would always remain beyond my understanding and in that moment, it was fine with me. When he sat down to rest, I was transported back to my familiar realm. The women wiped my stomach, which revealed no scar, pulled my clothing together and helped me off the table. My legs felt slightly shaky as they touched the floor and I stepped over to the side and leaned against the wall while the next patient approached the table. It was Lois, and she shoved my camera into my hands and said, "Here, Andrea. Quick! Take pictures."

Feeling quite frazzled, with my shorts not even buttoned all the way up, I obediently started snapping pictures, hoping that I was pointing the camera in the right direction. Alex worked again on her neck, swiftly removing more of the long stringy substance. He held it up to show me before dropping it into the bowl. Although I could clearly see that the substance was real, I felt all my doubts come pouring back into my mind. Somehow, it had been easier to relax into my own healing than to accept

Lois's, which I could see much more clearly. She was closed up and off the table in about thirty seconds.

After operating on five or six more people, Alex stopped, dipped his hands into some clean water and left the room. Mary informed me that it was time to take a break before the second half of the session. I was relieved because it was hot and sticky in that small area and after what I had just been through, I needed to get out of there. I felt light-headed. My shoes seemed padded, my feet not quite making contact with the ground. Lois grabbed my hand.

"We got some great pictures! How do you feel?" she asked me.

"I'm not sure. . . . My stomachache is gone," I answered.

"My neck feels terrific! Come on! I can hardly wait to have a talk with Alex." Lois propelled me toward a corridor where Alex's office was located.

She knocked and we heard a voice call out, "Yah. Come in."

We slid the curtained glass door aside and there he was, looking small and unimposing, exactly as he had looked the day before. He was sitting behind his desk, puffing away on a cigarette and he greeted us with a big smile. I was relieved by the coolness of the air conditioning and sat down to catch my breath.

"So. Today you have watched many operations. What do you think about this spiritual healing?" he asked me.

What could I say to him? Could I tell him that my brain was freaking out from too much data, that I was on overload, that all of my belief systems had been smashed in an hour and a half of his average day?

"I think it's wonderful," I clumsily replied. "How did you know what was wrong with me?"

"The Holy Spirit is the One Who knows. He does the work. I am only the instrument. I am a simple human being, just like you. But I know my spiritual obligation to this world and I allow the Holy Spirit to use my body to do His work."

His quality of attention and the sound of his voice relaxed me. I leaned back in my chair to listen.

"You see, we have two kinds of bodies, the material and the spiritual. When they are separate, the world is dark. The two bodies must be in tune to be healthy, so we must keep them clean and balanced. Doctors operate on the material body, removing obstructions to the physical energy flow. Spiritual healers remove obstructions, but we also infuse the body with energy that continues healing long after we have finished the operation. Food for the material body grows on the earth, but food for the spiritual body comes from God. I am a channel for God's healing vibrations."

"Can you see inside of me?" I asked.

"Yes, I can see, but I also feel different levels of vibrations in the body. Wherever illness collects, the vibrations become very dense. Before I operate, I close my eyes and my hands become like a magnet. They are attracted to the area where the sickness has manifested."

I had noticed that brief moment before each operation when Alex closed his eyes and laid his hands over the body.

He continued. "The body is the home of the spirit. The heart and soul are the doors and the mind is the window. Sometimes we cannot sleep at night because we are worried about so many things. We have left the window open and we are traveling outside of our spirit home. The negative vibrations float in through the window and we become unhappy. We begin to have negative thoughts and then we think if we have a small pain, we must have cancer. That thought becomes a sickness. Since all sickness begins in the mind, the goal of the healer is to strengthen the people spiritually so that they will be strong enough to close the window of the mind. Sometimes, it is hard to make the mind cooperate because it is stubborn. Then, we do the operation. When we enter the body through the door, we infuse healing energy to open the heart and strengthen the soul. Now the material mind will take a holiday and the patient will be guided by the feelings in the heart and soul. Once we have developed a stronger spiritual mind, the negative vibrations leave through the window, the same way they came in.

"So many people come here from foreign countries because they have heard about these miracles, but their minds are weak and they cannot believe," he continued. "But it is not the job of the healer to convince the people. It is the job of the healer to heal the people."

He leaned back in his chair, took a big drag on his cigarette and placed it in the ashtray. Up until now, I had always had judgments about smoking and people who smoked. But with Alex, there was something almost gratifying about seeing him smoke. It really blew a hole in the righteous concepts that many people, including myself, held about spirituality. It seemed to have become a common practice to use a person's habits as a yardstick to measure how evolved they may or may not be. Here was one of the clearest, most spiritual human beings I had ever come in contact with, smoking up a storm.

"Now I will rest before I do more healing. I think there are many sick people today," he said.

We thanked him for his time, and he and Lois embraced. As we left the room, I looked back and saw Alex lean forward to rest his head in his delicate hands, like a child in grade school taking a nap at recess.

After a twenty-minute break, the healing reconvened as before and I watched Alex operate on at least a hundred more people. He worked on them one after the other, with only seconds between operations. If I had considered the possibility of his faking the work, I now had to drop that. There simply wasn't time to hide anything up his sleeves while working so continuously at that pace. I just couldn't explain what was happening and I really wanted to be able to.

He seemed inexhaustible, blessing people, cleaning their blood, and removing all kinds of strange-looking material from their diseased bodies. When he was finally through, he collapsed back in his chair and said, "Finished!" Washing his hands with fresh water, he slowly walked out of the healing room, looking frail and spent. He hobbled shakily on his high-heeled shoes into his office, and closed the door behind him. We sat down to wait in the outer office.

In just a few minutes he emerged, looking totally revitalized, and walked out to sit beside me. I expected that he would hardly be able to speak, but he looked as if he had had a full night's sleep.

"We will talk a little bit," he said.

"Alex, you're glowing. Don't you get tired after seeing all those people?" Lois asked.

"Yes, I get very tired. But after the healing, I meditate and ask the Holy Spirit to give me energy so that I can talk to the people, and I become refreshed immediately." He flashed us a big smile. "Every night before I sleep, I breathe deeply and slowly and I pray to God to give me strength. I say 'Thank you, God, for You are the One to give me a strong body and a clear mind.'

"Every morning when I wake up, I look in the mirror and I smile to myself. I smile to my body, my organs, and my mind. Then I am ready to be with my family and friends. If you don't know how to smile, everyone will be angry at you. If you smile at the world, the world will smile back and you will always be healthy and happy. You know, we remember to give a holiday to the body, but we forget about the spirit. When I relax, breathe deeply, and meditate, I am giving my spiritual body a holiday."

He took my hand in his. "Maybe you have some questions," he suggested.

I had many. "How do you go inside the body?" I asked him. "It seems an impossible thing to do."

"The Holy Spirit is the One to go in. I have seven spirit guides who direct me. My left hand is the material hand. It makes the opening, controls the flow of the blood and sends out anesthesia so that the patient feels no pain. The right is the spiritual hand in which I hold a wet cotton ball and squeeze out water while the opening is made. When I use water, it is easier for me to enter the body because water is the symbol of life, a gift from spirit. After the body is open, I do not have to go very deeply inside because the right hand becomes a magnet, drawing out the diseased tissue."

I must have looked completely overwhelmed because Alex stopped his explanations and regarded me as if I were a child. "This is all very new for you because they do not yet do this kind of healing in your country. It is time for you to relax and meditate on these things that I have told you."

He put his arms around me, sweetly touched his cheek to mine, and got up to greet other people who were waiting to see him.

On the way out, I noticed a wooden donation box resting on an outdoor reception desk. People dropped money in as they passed, some giving large bills and others a few coins. I asked Lois how much I should offer and she told me that it was up to me. I felt uncomfortable because I really had no idea how much to give. I hardly knew what had even happened, much less how to decide what it was worth monetarily. How could I put a price on what I had just experienced? I reached into my wallet, pulled out a twenty-dollar bill and dropped it into the box. A woman who was sitting at the desk thanked me and asked me if I would like some holy oil that had been blessed by Alex. Of course, I said I would. While I was thanking the woman, I was drawn to a book she was selling called *The Truth Behind Faith Healing in the Philippines* by Jaime T. Licauco. I scanned it quickly and saw that it contained photographs of various healers and answered the most basic questions about the many different forms of faith healing. It seemed coherent and informative, so I purchased it.

"I've been writing to the author of that book," Lois commented. "We'll probably get a chance to meet him while we're here."

We hailed a taxi and took another death-defying ride

through the streets of Manila back to our hotel where I retired to my bed, ready to make the world stop for a few minutes so I could get my bearings.

Energy pulses were running through my body and my mind was a mass of confusion. I checked my stomach every few minutes, to verify what had happened to me. A tiny red mark was all the evidence that remained. I knew that what I had seen was undeniably real, but my mind kept telling me that it was impossible. I was hopelessly groping to make contact with a familiar place in my head that seemed to have vanished. It was as if something alien had gotten into the works and the programs were being rearranged in a way that was unidentifiable. The language I had always used to define things was scrambled and I had no mental frame of reference, nothing to hold on to. There seemed to be no place to file this new information where it made any sense, no way to put it in order. I felt that the security of all that I believed was melting away and the inside of my head was nothing more than mush.

I had always believed that flesh was a dense form of matter that could not be penetrated by the mere hands and will of a human being. And now, even after I had seen it to be otherwise, I was still desperately trying to preserve this belief and prove it right. But my direct experience was creating a new arena in which the old ideas were too weak to hold their own. The energetic heat of a new and potent reality was melting my beliefs into the abstract stuff from which they had been formed. My head felt like an incinerator, pulsing and throbbing as it burnt up the old and made room for the new. Nothing seemed solid or permanent. All that I knew for sure was what I felt in my heart. I trusted Alex and felt that what he was doing was good.

I turned to the book I had just purchased. Perhaps it would hold some answers for me. I glanced at the author's name, Jaime T. Licauco, and the face of a Filipino man quickly flashed into my mind's eye. He looked vaguely familiar but I could not study him, because it was only a fleeting image that quickly disappeared. I opened to the introduction but before I could get through the first paragraph, the book dropped to my chest and I dozed off into a dream.

I am standing in a book store, with a young boy who has grasped me by the seat of my pants and is holding on as hard as he can. I grab his hair, pulling it painfully, and tell him that if he will let go, so will I. We both do so simultaneously but almost immediately, he attaches himself to my body once again. He tells me that he wants me to love him. As I contemplate what this means, I sense some strange energy. I see people gathering around who are alien and dark. I am in a frequency that feels dense, thick, and needy. I want to be free of it. Suddenly the awareness hits me that I must be dreaming and I have the power to remove myself from this place if I so wish. A feeling of great relief fills me as I begin to lift my body from the earth, raising myself out of this undesirable dimension.

Now, I am rapidly moving through space, completely aware that I am in a dream state of astral flight. It is by far the most blissful feeling that I can ever recall. As I fly, I see white energy patterns moving through the atmosphere. I use my arms as wings and can raise and lower myself at will. I ecstatically soar straight between trees and houses as I make my way to Lois, for I want to show her what I can do.

I look down from the sky to try to find her, but she is not beneath me. When I look straight ahead, I see her, standing directly across from me, ten feet off the ground. I realize that this is the realm where she exists naturally and this is the first time that I have ever been here. I feel humbled as I look at her.

Lois informs me that it is almost morning and I will soon be returning to my body. She suggests that I take this opportunity to carefully observe everything in detail as it exists in this particular dimension. I gently touch down to earth and begin to walk around, paying careful attention to all that I see.

I am starting to feel heavy and I try to lift back into the air, but I am disappointed because I can raise up only a few feet. I pass sleeping bodies lining my pathway. I see that these body temples have been carelessly left here while the spirits are blissfully traveling in the astral dream planes. They are open and vulnerable and I suddenly realize that I have also left my physical body somewhere with no protection. I send a beam of white healing light to surround my sleeping form, ask to remember the important lessons I have been given by this dream, and prepare to awaken.

When I opened my eyes, I quickly glanced over at Lois, half expecting her to be levitated several feet. There she was napping, and to my relief, she and her bed were still earthbound. I lay back and reviewed the dream.

The young boy who kept attaching himself to me seemed to be a symbol for the old beliefs that would not simply fall away at will. Even when I thought I had released them, they returned, reattaching themselves. It seemed I would never be able to rid myself of them. But release comes from love and understanding, and when I realized that I was functioning in a lower level of awareness, I knew I could change. When I raised my consciousness, the old ideas fell away and I was light enough to fly.

Once in this elevated state, I could see how Lois functioned in her daily existence, that she lived in this higher awareness as a normal way of life. And in her wisdom, she had not tried to teach me about it. She had simply exposed me to a new reality and allowed me to accept it for myself.

The bodies lying unattended reminded me of Alex's words about the body being a home and the mind a window. I had left my home with the window open and while I carelessly flew about in the astral realms of doubt, my home (my body) and my heart were vulnerable to any kind of negativity that desired entry. I decided that each night before sleep, it would be a good idea to mentally program a constant connection with my emotional and physical needs.

The steady rhythm of Lois's breath reminded me of the rest of her life. She was always so peaceful. Nothing ever seemed to bother her. She just took everything in her stride. I sighed, wondering if I would ever be that way.

The dream had left me feeling lighter and far less upset. Now I could return to my book and my search for answers. I reached for my meditation crystal which I had brought from home. It helped me to concentrate so I held it in my hand while I read.

5

SHEDDING
LIGHT

When the phone rang, I was so deeply engrossed in reading that I paid very little attention to Lois's conversation. She hung up and said, "I have something to tell you that's going to really interest you."

I looked up.

"Jaime Licauco, the author of that book you're reading, just called from the lobby and he's on his way up. Not a bad piece of timing, eh?"

I was thrilled. Everything seemed to be happening perfectly.

In a few moments, a small, olive-skinned man arrived, shook hands with Lois, and with a very unassuming walk, went to take a seat in a chair in the corner. He was smiling shyly and his narrow eyes and yellow skin tone gave him the aspect of a Chinese, although he was definitely Filipino. I couldn't stop staring at him because I recognized him. His was the face I had "seen" in that brief moment just before I opened his book!

We were politely introduced and he and Lois chatted for a while. He spoke English so beautifully that it was hard to believe it was his second language. Lois explained why we were here and thanked him for his books, which she had found helpful and interesting. He turned to look at me and we locked eyes in a surprisingly intense stare. Then he looked away and, expressing himself with the eloquence of a scholar, began to talk about himself.

"I was a businessman, working for many years in the field of human resources and social development. In 1976, a French woman visiting the Philippines invited me to observe a psychic surgeon at work. Although I had never seen one before, it was with some reluctance that I accepted her offer, because I had always been a skeptic. I was a rational-minded man with a healthy respect for science and conventional medicine. I simply did not believe in these paranormal things.

"I was amazed at what I saw but I still felt reluctant to accept the reality of faith healing. You see, my belief structures were so firmly rooted that I tried to deny the truth of what I had seen with my own eyes. But, after my first exposure, something started to happen in my mind. A sort of reshaping had begun and I couldn't stop thinking about what I had seen. I felt moved, and I was compelled to research the validity of these demonstrations. I eventually became convinced that psychic surgery is real and that there are things that cannot be explained in modern scientific terms. However, something within my brain still will not allow me to blindly accept what I see.

"There is a rich world of psychic phenomena prevalent in the Philippines which seems to be unequalled anywhere else in the world. It fascinates me beyond description. In my attempts to prove to myself the validity and at times the nonvalidity of these occurrences, I have fallen into a world from which there seems to be no return. In fact, I will soon be starting a paranormal research society in order to delve even deeper into these realities. I guess I'm hooked!" He half-nervously laughed at himself, and once again our eyes met.

"Who are you?" he asked me quite directly.

I told him about my connection with Lois and my fascination

with the photographs that had eventually brought me here to see the healers for myself. While I talked, I noticed that Jaime had begun to smile, something that he did not do frivolously. He seemed fascinated with the quartz crystal that I was rhythmically turning over and over in my hand as I spoke.

We spent a very pleasant evening, sharing information about the Philippines and our various metaphysical experiences. I enjoyed the combination of his personal shyness and his eagerness to discuss intimate things that had been deeply moving him for the last six years. He seemed almost starved for the opportunity to share these parts of himself. When he rose to leave, Lois and I got up to say goodbye and I felt compelled to hug him. As I did, I spontaneously handed him the crystal.

"Please accept this as a gift. When you hold it in your hand, it will balance you. I would really like you to have it," I said.

His eyes watered and he reached out to receive the crystal. "You are the one that I was told about. I felt the energy when I walked into the room. Would you meet with me for dinner tomorrow night?"

Quite surprised, I consented and he left.

Lois and I turned to each other in amazement, shrugged our shoulders and laughed.

"This place is like the psycho ward. Let's order some dessert," she said.

We drowned our confusion in a couple of hot fudge sundaes and talked late into the night.

"One year ago, I was foretold of your arrival in my life," Jaime told me. He smiled gently. "By the way, my friends call me Jimmy."

We were having dinner in a small café near the hotel. We sat at a table that was tucked away in the corner and Jimmy was holding the crystal that I had given him. He was eager to share his story with me.

"I met an American woman last year who had a quartz

crystal similar to this one. She asked me if I had ever held one and felt its energy. I had not, so she offered to let me hold hers. I took it into my hand and I experienced a thrilling rush of energy that became so strong, I actually left my body, which collapsed on the floor. While I was floating in this state I call astral projection, I heard voices that told me that within one year, another woman would appear and would give me a crystal. I wondered who it would be but after a while I began to doubt that I had ever really heard those voices. When Lois called, I felt a strong urge to come and meet with her. Then I met you. I felt an immediate connection with you, even before you handed me the crystal. Although we had obviously never met before, you seemed so familar to me."

I had also felt the connection and I told him about seeing his face just before I opened his book. It seemed like such an obvious cliché, but I really felt as if I had known him before. We both agreed that we must have had a connection in another lifetime, because of the familiarity with each other that we both felt. We chatted for a while, and for the first time since I had landed on Asian shores, my surroundings seemed familiar and relaxing. The café was cozy and warm, with a definite European flavor. The smells were unusually Western and strains of classical music were floating through the air. The fact that we could have been anywhere made this meeting even more interesting.

"You Filipinos are such an amazing race of people," I said. "You seem to be so powerfully connected to spiritual things. Back in America, especially in Southern California, there are hordes of people enrolling in metaphysical classes, trying to teach themselves to tune in to the energy of crystals and to leave their bodies. Students practice for years, hoping that some day, they'll be able to astral project. But here, someone simply hands you a crystal for the first time and you float away and hear voices."

We both had a good laugh and Jimmy shook his head in bewilderment. He didn't know what to make of it either. He thought it might be something about the way Filipinos are raised, with strong support for accepting unusual happenings. But he had actually been a nonbeliever until he had had some experiences that forced him to change his mind. We discussed the possibility of there being something inherent in the land that affected one's connection with other dimensions.

The waiter brought steaming bowls of soup and rice to our table. We were both hungry and happy that the food was there. A feeling of contentment filled me for the first time since I had arrived in the Philippines. It was so easy to communicate with Jimmy. I felt no culture gap, so I could relax and speak without wondering if I were being misunderstood. I was strangely at ease with him and it was a great relief to finally have someone to open up to who might be able to shed some light on the happenings that puzzled me so.

At first we ate in silence, placing our full attention on the savory fish soup. After a few moments, I stopped eating and asked him, "What is the difference between psychic surgery and faith healing?"

With his long tapered fingers, Jimmy delicately placed his spoon by his bowl. "Faith healing is a general term that includes all the forms of spiritual healing. Psychic surgery is only one of the many methods that fall under this heading. The term comes from the fact that the healers utilize their faith in a higher power to guide them in their healing practices." He paused. "This café is known for its exotic teas. I'll order some for us."

I nodded. "Jimmy, I watched Alex do more than a hundred operations. I saw it with my own eyes but I just can't figure out what he's doing. Is there a real explanation or do we just have to accept it as a miracle?"

Jimmy smiled and leaned forward, speaking in a whisper as if he feared being overheard. "Andrea, I've been watching these things for over ten years and I still find myself doubting their reality." He leaned back and sighed with relief that he had just revealed the deep dark secret of his own doubts.

"You see," he continued, "psychic surgery is so spectacular and effective, that even if you just watch, it will crack open the beliefs and ideas of the most headstrong of people—even me," he added with a laugh. "I've done a lot of thinking about it and I will try to tell you what I think is happening on a physical level during one of these material operations." He reached across the table and took my hand in his.

"As we know, the human body is not a solid mass." He pressed my skin between the palms of his hands as if to demonstrate his point. "It is a vibrating molecular structure of separate moving and living cells. The molecules of our flesh are held together by an electromagnetic force field which vibrates at such a high frequency, it appears and feels solid. Through many years of practice at concentration and meditation, the healers have the ability to alter their vibratory rates at will. When they are about to do an operation, they quicken their vibration by moving into a deep, almost trance-like state. You must have observed this in Alex. He is able to channel a shot of energy through his body that is like a laser beam. He sends it out of his hands and into the body of the patient.

"This high-intensity frequency displaces the denser frequency of the electromagnetic force field which holds human flesh together. Without their magnetic adhesion, the cells separate, and an opening is created into which his hand sinks. The left hand remains inside the opening at all times, continuously sending out the laser-like frequency. This keeps the flesh open.

"The operation is painless because a natural anesthesia seems to pour out of his hands while he works. His right hand acts like a magnet, drawing up the diseased tissue and then removing it. When he has finished, he takes his hands away. The magnetic field returns to normal, and the cells interlock as they originally were. There is no scar because no real incision was made."

The things that he was telling me sounded logical, yet when I saw the theories in practice, they were so hard to believe.

The strong aroma of jasmine caught our attention and Jimmy

suddenly let go of my hand. I had hardly noticed that he was still holding it because I felt so comfortable with him. He looked slightly embarrassed while the waiter cleared the table to make room for our tea. I held the cup between my hands, allowing the smell to fill my nostrils.

"Why don't they just analyze the material that was removed and prove it once and for all?" I asked.

"It has been analyzed many times," he told me.

"Well, then, why doesn't everyone believe it?"

Jimmy casually stirred four heaping teaspoonfuls of sugar into his tea. I grimaced at the saccharine mixture that he was making, but he seemed to enjoy the taste immensely.

"Because people aren't always honest. In certain cases, they took the tissue and switched it to animal tissue just to discredit the healers. It was very humiliating for them and they became hurt and disillusioned. They decided to stop allowing people to keep the extracted matter, stating that a healer's job is only to heal and if their decision to withhold the material disturbed anyone, that was not their problem."

"But why would people rather believe the negative findings if there were positive ones, too?"

Jimmy sipped his tea and frowned. "Some people try to deny psychic surgery because they are afraid of shaking their safe little worlds. They would rather believe that all healers are charlatans and, unfortunately, there are many. Some of them get really good at sleight of hand and magic but they have been caught hiding things up their sleeves and under tables. These fakes use chicken parts, animal blood, anything they can find, to make money and to deceive people. They are just insecure people who make their livings by trying to invalidate things that they cannot understand.

"And then, there is a further complication that is difficult to explain because it is one of the greatest mysteries of all. I don't know if you would accept it."

"I would like to try," I told him.

Jimmy looked straight into my eyes as if he were forcefully engaging my attention. I felt my face flush and I wondered why he was staring at me so intensely. Then he spoke.

"The healers are able to materialize, to make an illness appear in the physical while it is still only a thought form. They feel that all illness begins in the patient's mind. They can tap into these unconscious thoughts and materialize them into a physical form and then remove them. So they can heal an illness that hasn't even appeared yet. When people have tried to analyze this materialized tissue, sometimes the findings are confusing. It doesn't always check out as something real. There are even cases where the tissue has disappeared. By the time it reached the lab, the container was empty."

"But if many of the analyses have been positive, why haven't those findings been publicized?"

Jimmy grimaced. "Look what these few days have done to you. Do you think that most people are ready to shake up their worlds like you and I have done? This is why more energy goes into exposing the charlatans than into support for the healers who are doing the real work. Of course, ridding the healing world of the fakes is an extremely important effort. So many people who come to the Philippines for help run into these fakes and are seriously robbed and deceived. It is a tragic situation because their bad experiences will sour them against the only hope they may have left. But it is a pity that the real healers receive so little publicity for the good that they do."

I mentioned that most Westerners, even if they wanted to believe in alternate realities, have no background to support their doing so.

"We in the Philippines have a different orientation. But there was a time when events such as psychic surgery and spirit contact baffled even the people to whom they were happening. In 1901, a group of courageous individuals who were spontaneously involved in communicating with the spirit world organized themselves. Did you notice the banner hanging in Alex's healing room? It says UNION ESPIRITISTA CRISTIANA DE PILIPINAS. This

Rev. Alex Orbito and me.

*Rev. Alex Orbito
praying before
healing.*

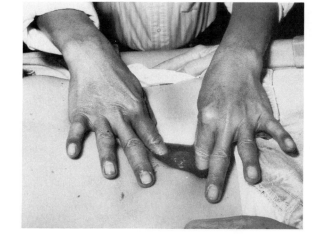

*Rev. Alex Orbito
performing stomach
surgery on me.*

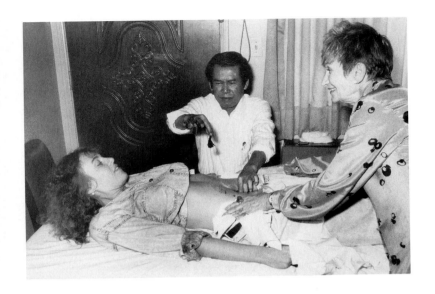

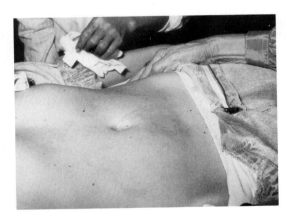

Rev. Alex Orbito holding blood clots he has removed from my stomach.

My stomach immediately after operation.

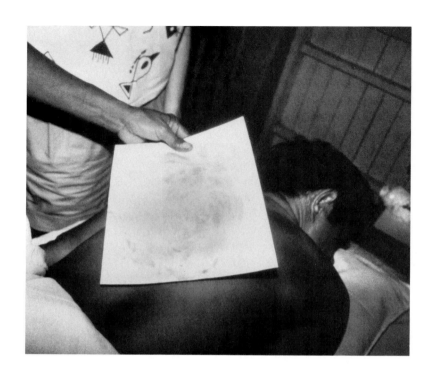

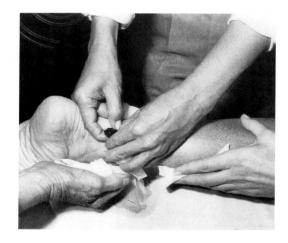

"Spirit" x-ray etched in oil created by healer applying magnetic energy.

Rev. Alex Orbito doing psychic operation on foot.

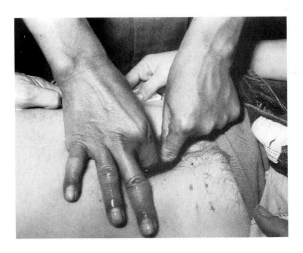

Rev. Alex Orbito performing psychic surgery.

Rev. Alex Orbito removing cancerous tumor.

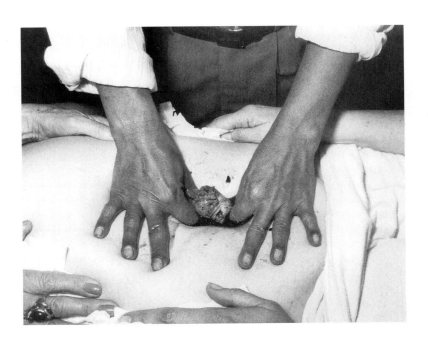

Jaime Licauco (Jimmy).

Here I am on the road to Mt. Banahaw The mountain is partially covered by cloud formations.

Some of the pools at Santa Lucia—Mt. Banahaw.

Me standing under a waterfall at Santa Lucia—Mt. Banahaw.

The Crown of Stone—Mt. Banahaw.

Here I am climbing up from the water in the cave of Jacob's Well at Mt. Banahaw.

means Union of Philippine Christian Spiritists, an organization that was formed and acts as a support group for spiritual development. It is through this union that we were first able to conduct research without encountering resistance.

"There are many local chapters still active today, holding meetings on Sundays. That's tomorrow evening. Perhaps you and Lois would like to attend? You might see some things that you have never seen before."

"Undoubtedly," I commented, laughing out loud.

We became silent and just sat for several moments, looking into each others eyes. For a brief instant, I felt the memories of a thousand years of a past that we shared. These pictures were unclear, as if behind a veil, yet they were undeniably there and we both knew it. We sat in the café until it closed, having totally lost track of time.

On the way home, Jimmy turned to me and said, "I would like to bring you to Mount Banahaw. It is an enchanted sacred mountain, filled with high spiritual energy. I feel that you will respond to this place in the way that I have. People go there to renew their strength, increase their psychic awareness and learn about other dimensions. Sometimes, we even sleep in the caves. Would you like to go?"

"Oh, I'd love to. When are you going? I have plans to go to the province of Pangasinan in a couple of days. Lois says that there are some very interesting healers there."

"Yes. That is a very important place for you to visit. But it will not interfere with Mount Banahaw. I am going next weekend with my good friend, Boy Fajardo. He's a businessman but he is also an *herbulario*. That's a native folk healer who uses reflexology, acupressure, herbs, and massage. Boy lives in Manila with his family and he also maintains a house at the foothills of the mountain."

I beamed. "Why do they call him Boy?"

"Oh, that is a Philippine custom. It is a name often given to the first son. It's like calling someone Junior."

We had arrived back at my hotel. I thanked him for being

so open with me. He wished me a good journey into the province, smiled, waved, and was gone.

I walked through the revolving doors and when I caught my reflection in the glass, the pair of eyes looking back at me held a new depth. I was changing dramatically each day, and this night I felt I had been profoundly touched by my own ancient past. Spiritist meetings and enchanted mountains were next on the list.

6

MEEJUM
MESSAGES

Lois and I were not in a hurry, but apparently the taxi driver was. On this wet and sultry Sunday evening, we were being sped to one of the local chapters for a monthly meeting of the Espiritistas. The pouring rain did not seem to inhibit our taxi's flight, and in record time, we were dropped off at the corner of a dark street. We stepped out into a steamy downpour and scurried toward an old, weather-beaten house marked by a small black and white sign that read UNION ESPIRITISTA CRISTIANA DE PILIPINAS. Following a hand-drawn arrow that pointed to the back of the house, we splashed down the walkway, drenched by both the falling rain and the perspiration on our flushed faces. We were met at a badly torn screen door by a small, dark woman wearing a conservative high-necked dress and a pair of rubber clogs.

"Welcome to my center, *seesters,*" she sang proudly. "My name is Alita Rosario.* I am happy to be your hostess this evening. Come and meet all the *seesters* and brothers."

*This name has been changed to protect the individual's privacy.

We shook the weather out of our hair and entered a large square room set up with folding chairs and lit by a few harsh light bulbs suspended from the ceiling. Alita led us to two women who looked as old as the sea, fanning themselves with pieces of paper.

"These are our visiting clairvoyants," Alita informed us. "They belong to another center but they wanted to spend this evening with us because they knew you would be coming. They do not speak much English."

I was about to ask how they could possibly know we would be here, since we had decided to come only a few hours earlier. Then I realized that Alita had called them clairvoyants. Maybe they knew before we did. They greeted us with their ancient toothless smiles. We shook hands and, although we could not speak with each other, I felt them reaching out to welcome us. They closed their eyes and as we walked away, I could hear a muffled snore escaping from one of them.

We spent the next fifteen minutes greeting the forty-odd Spiritist members who had gathered at Alita's center. Her banner hung proudly at the front of the room, its purple and gold letters framing the image of a white dove flying downward with its wings spread. I had seen this same dove on Alex's banner. It was the symbol of the messenger of the Holy Spirit bringing the healing light to earth. On the walls were photographs of several of the past presidents of the Espiritistas, but one particular face caught my eye. His name was Guillermo Tolentino, and I read a short piece of information that was posted by his picture. He had been president of the Espiritistas in 1926, besides being one of the greatest sculptors the Philippines had ever known. He was responsible for a great deal of the research that was later done on the first known psychic surgeon, Eleuterio Terte. Tolentino had written his personal interpretation of the founding principles of the Espiritistas:

God is my father. Nature is my mother. The Universe is my way. Eternity is my kingdom. Immortality is my life.

The mind is my house. Truth is my worship. Love is my law. Form is my manifestation. Conscience is my guide. Peace is my shelter. Experience is my school. Obstacle is my lesson. Difficulty is my stimulant. Joy is my hymn. Pain is my warning. Work is my blessing. Light is my realization. Friend is my companion. Struggle is my opportunity. Future time is my promise. Equilibrium is my attitude. Order is my path. Beauty is my ideal. Perfection is my destiny.

Alita stood at the front of the room, asking for our attention. Everyone rose while she prayed and invited the spirits to join us. During her invocation, a large cockroach dropped from the ceiling, landing on the face of the snoring clairvoyant. She awoke from her sleep, lazily flicked away the bug, and, after letting out a spontaneous burp, rose and joined in the prayers. Lois and I stood to pray in front of a couple of empty seats. Besides the sound of the rain hitting the roof of the house, all that could be heard were the utterings of prayer. I watched various people begin to sway in slow motion. A silent rhythmical sound seemed to float around the room, and all who moved did so in unison. When the prayers were finished, Alita opened her eyes and asked everyone to be seated. Several people continued swaying in their seats, already in a deep trance-like state. Alita spoke for a few minutes, welcoming everyone and letting us know how proud and happy she was that Lois and I were here to learn more about the ways of spiritual life in the Philippines.

"We will now hear from the spirit world and receive a message for our foreign friends," she said.

Alita turned toward her banner, placed her hands on the fringe that hung from the bottom and stood silently. Several old women stood up and surrounded her as her body began to undulate. Her movements became fuller and more exaggerated and I began to feel a dizziness in my stomach. Suddenly Alita collapsed in the arms of a very old and wrinkled woman standing directly beside her. She was placed in a chair, her head resting on the table in front of her. She remained there for several moments, not moving, while I breathed deeply, trying to settle my stomach pains.

With my hands on my abdomen, I seemed to see electricity begin to course through Alita's body. Two large dogs that had been sleeping outside started barking at the top of their lungs, but the intruding sound did not seem to concern anyone. Alita lifted her head with her eyes still closed, and tilted it in my direction. I felt exposed, as though she were looking straight through me. She raised her right hand, and it waved continuously as she spoke. She uttered words in Tagalog with a loud, low resonance that did not even slightly resemble her modest, high-pitched speaking voice. The women were sitting very close to her, dutifully writing down every word. Doing the best I could to control my nausea, I sat there, fascinated, watching this woman who was in a deep trance, seemingly possessed by a spirit from another dimension. After about ten minutes, the voice stopped, she closed her mouth, and slowly sank down out of her chair, landing on the hard floor beneath her with a loud bang. I felt it in my own body.

The women raised Alita from the floor and led her to a chair at the back of the room. They sat her down and began to gently massage her head and solar plexus, snapping their fingers around her forehead until she opened her eyes, half-dazed, and looked around. She got her bearings and smiled reassuringly at us. I noticed that my nausea was letting up a bit and I hoped that the pains would soon stop.

Now a young child of about ten got up and bashfully walked to the front of the room, seating himself in Alita's chair. The women gathered round him and prayed while he closed his eyes. His body went into the same trance-like sway that Alita's had and I grabbed my stomach. The pains were back in full force and this time, I broke out into a cold sweat. The more he moved in his seat, the more nauseous I became. The room began to swirl around me and I went completely off-balance, not knowing if I was sitting in my chair or standing on my head. No matter how hard I breathed, the dizziness would not let up and the nausea was becoming unbearable. Through my fogged-over vision, I spotted a bathroom in the corner and just as I was about to make a run for it, the child began to speak.

A loud booming voice shocked me into stillness. It was as if a very large, old man in the body of a young child were preaching to an enormous congregation. He gestured broadly with his hands while he spoke and although the language was foreign to me, I felt the power of the message. His words reached my ears as if I were in the bottom of a well, the lower notes reverberating in my stomach. I wondered if I would ever regain my equilibrium. After what felt like forever, the child quieted down. His head slowly rolled forward until it rested gently on the table in front of him. That was my cue.

"I'm sick," I told Lois. I somehow managed to stand up on my feet and run into the bathroom. She followed close behind me. The walls of the room were closing in and spinning round and round. I tried to vomit, but I couldn't.

"I have to get out of here," I moaned.

"Let's go," Lois said. She asked someone to call a taxi. Alita scurried around, making arrangements for us. My humiliation at attracting attention was far overshadowed by the pain I was feeling.

In my crouched position, I saw a pair of clogged feet that looked like roots. I gazed up and saw a short, concerned-looking man quietly talking with Lois.

He stooped down, placed a warm hand on my stomach and looked into my eyes. "I will come back to your hotel and take care of you," he informed me. I nodded without asking any questions. He took my hand and led me outside to a waiting taxi. Doubled over with pain, I climbed in. The three of us took off for the hotel.

"I will take X ray. Do you have holy oil?" I was warmly tucked in my bed, still quite nauseous but relieved to be back in my own territory. Lois scurried around, gathering certain materials under this man's direction: holy oil, a sheet of white hotel stationery, a white towel, and a Bible.

"This is Camilo Mirande," Lois told me. "I met him last year at Alex's place. We are lucky he was there tonight. He'll take good care of you."

"First we pray," he told us. He and Lois recited the Lord's Prayer while I moaned. Then he pulled back the covers of the bed. He rubbed the holy oil on my stomach, laid the stationery over it and then the white towel. With his hands on top, he instructed me to breathe deeply three times, allowing my stomach to move against his hand. I did so with great difficulty, and when I was through, he removed his hands, the towel, and the paper. When he held the paper up to the light, there was an X-ray-like picture of my intestines, etched in oil! Along the right side was a dark spot which he pointed to with his creature-like fingers. I was too uncomfortable to be amazed. Lois took a photograph.

"That is a gas pocket, the material cause for your pain. We will discuss the spiritual cause later. Now I will do an operation. Do you have cotton?"

I had a few cotton balls in a manicure set, and I told Lois where to find them. Camilo took a cotton ball in his hand, dipped it in water, knelt down beside me, and continued to pray. He then squeezed the cotton ball onto my stomach, placed his hands on the wet skin, and before I knew it, his fingers had dipped inside. He immersed his hands up to the wrist and began to make squishing movements, stirring me up like a large pot of stew.

"I am cleaning your blood," he informed me casually. Camilo was missing some of his most crucial teeth so when he spoke, I had to listen very carefully. He kept removing the cotton ball and squeezing liquid out of it, then placing it back inside the opening. Continuing the motions for a few more seconds, he then removed his hands and discarded the used cotton. He wiped a small amount of blood off my stomach and winked at me. "We are not yet finished," he said.

He took another piece of paper and repeated the X-ray procedure. When he held the new X ray up to the light, it looked almost identical to the first except the black spot was gone. He nodded his approval, and grabbing another cotton ball, dipped it into holy oil and placed it over the area where he had just finished working. For a moment I couldn't tell what he was doing, until I saw the cotton moving straight through my skin until it had disappeared inside my body. I was shocked. Had he lost it? Would they have to rush me to the hospital to have it surgically removed?

It was as if he could read my mind. "I will take it out tomorrow. The holy oil will draw acid to the cotton overnight. Tonight you must rest and pray for faith. I know that you have seen too much in a very short time. Sleep and dream. You are being tested and I know you are strong enough to succeed. Good night. I will return in the morning."

I tried to grasp the reality of what he was telling me. Had he really just inserted a cotton ball through my skin? And now he was saying good night and leaving? I thought maybe we should talk about this.

"May we keep the X rays?" Lois asked him.

"Yes, but they are of the spirit and in a short time will disappear. You will have only two oily pieces of paper," he said with a chuckle.

We offered to order him some food but he declined. As he was walking out the door Lois managed to stuff carfare into his pocket. And he was gone. Lois and I looked at each other, hardly knowing what to say.

"Is the pain gone?" she asked me.

"No, but I'm not nauseous anymore."

Lois stroked my head for a few moments while I silently prayed that Camilo would make it home safely. What if he died before morning? What would happen to me? I might have to walk around for the rest of my life with a piece of cotton in my stomach.

Lois prepared herself for bed while I tried to clear my mind.

I felt so uncomfortable about everything. My stomach still hurt slightly, I had disrupted a spirit gathering, and caused a spectacle at the Espiritista meeting. I hoped that everyone would not be angry with me.

"Just relax," Lois called out from the bathroom. "Everything is fine. He'll be back just like he promised. Try to get some sleep, now."

I shut my eyes, breathing slowly to ease the dull ache in my stomach. How did Lois always stay so calm and collected? Compared to her, I usually felt like I was bouncing off the walls. I followed her advice, let my mind go, and fell asleep.

I know that I am at the home of my parents, yet I do not recognize my surroundings. I am flying through the house and a group of laughing children are watching me, fascinated. After landing from my flight, I walk into the next room and see my parents. I tell them that I am not really there, that I have astral traveled to them. In actuality, I tell them, I am in a hotel room in Manila. Of course, they do not believe me.

I feel disappointed that they cannot accept what I have told them. I walk back into the first room and fly for the children for a while. I contemplate heading back to my body in Manila, but know that I cannot leave because I want my parents to know that I really astral traveled here. I have a new plan. I return to the room where my parents are relaxing.

I ask them if people can fly. They tell me that they cannot. I suggest to them that if they saw me fly, then they might believe that it is possible. They agree. I now have their full attention. We walk outside together and I lift off and begin sailing up to the sky. I fly with tremendous ease and grace, totally enjoying myself. They are entranced. I make precision moves through large tree branches and neatly touch down. They are exhilarated and joyful at my demonstration. I now know that I have shown them that other realities exist. I feel satisfied and walk back into the house.

*The children are excited with my magical display and
they huddle around me. I know that I am about to awaken,
so I tell them I have another surprise for them. If they watch
carefully, they will see me disappear. I am the center of
attention as I sit on the floor in the middle of the room. I
feel the children's awe as I start a slow dissolve, entering
back into the density of my physical body.*

When I awakened, I could remember the dream in full detail.
It was a perfect reflection of the split that I was experiencing.
The rigid, frightened part of me, represented by my parents,
doubted and discounted all that was new and challenging. This
was a result of my conditioning and it made me feel like a
stranger in my own life. Yet the open part of me, symbolized
by the children, was willing to accept and celebrate whatever
came my way. This was my trust and spontaneity which allowed
me to feel right at home with all that was transpiring here. The
dream was encouraging because the old ideas finally did yield.
I could see that the only way to accept what I was being shown
was to release the old and become like a child again. Perhaps
Lois, who was much older than I, was more of a child than I
was.

The morning sun was shining through the window and I
suddenly remembered the previous night. I pulled back the
covers to stare at my stomach. It looked normal and the pain
was completely gone. One could never tell that there was a piece
of cotton sitting just under the skin, waiting to be removed. I
was beginning to doubt it myself, when a knock was heard at
the door.

"Good morning." Camilo Mirande smiled his toothless smile
and entered the room. Relief flooded through me. He had made
it back. Since I was no longer in pain, I could get a better look
at him. He was quite a bit older than Alex and even more
otherworldly. The lines in his leathery face were permanently
carved, like those of a Native American chief. He was carrying
a bag of fruit, which he handed to Lois.

He spoke almost unintelligibly and yet, somehow, I could understand everything he said. "This is a present for you, Seester Looee. It is our native fruits." Then he turned to me.

"No fruit for you today. Only ripe papaya. We will do healing first. Then we talk. Seester Looee, please help me."

I giggled in spite of myself. Every time he said Lois's name, it sounded like he was saying "Louie" and I pictured a fat old man smoking a cigar.

Camilo wasted no time. He knelt beside me, held the Bible, and bowed his head. Lois came over to assist him. After a short prayer, he handed her the Bible, closed his eyes, and began to move his hands on my stomach, locating the correct spot. He wiggled his fingers until the tips of them were slightly inserted into my intestinal area. It looked as if he were trying to grab something. Suddenly, his first finger and thumb emerged. Between them was the tip of a piece of cotton. He coaxed and pulled, while I watched the entire cotton ball slowly appear, hanging between his fingers like a half-burned marshmallow, the center stained black. He made a nasty face. "Acid," he stated.

He dropped it into a bowl and rubbed my skin with holy oil. His hands felt warm and soothing. I closed my eyes and took it in, feeling nurtured and safe. I could hardly believe what I had just seen, but I was so relieved that the cotton was out of my stomach. Camilo prayed over me, and his prayers were so moving that there was no question he was making contact with something beyond what I could perceive with my limited vision. He went into the bathroom to flush the cotton and wash his hands.

He bounced back into the room. "Now I will give Seester Looee spiritual massage. Please lie down." Lois was delighted and without hesitation, relaxed on the other bed. Camilo took his Bible and knelt next to Lois, quietly uttering some strange words. He held the Bible over her head and suddenly his hands began to shake. He put the Bible down and passed his hands over her body, an inch or so away from making actual contact. The longer he worked, the more he shook, until Lois started shaking also. It looked like an earthquake happening on the other side of the room. It struck me so funny, I nearly giggled out loud, and then it all stopped as suddenly as it had started. Lois actually did laugh and Camilo smiled broadly, showing lots of gum and nodding his head.

"Camilo, I have never shaken like this before," Lois said breathlessly. "What happened?"

Camilo paused quietly, as if he were listening to something, and then announced without hesitation, "You will be fat!"

Lois stared at him incredulously and I burst out laughing.

"What did you say?" she asked.

"Yes, Seester, you will be fat," he repeated. "You are very powerful and your body is too small to handle so much energy. But don't worry. The Spirit will take care of it."

"But I don't want to be fat," she objected. "I've never been fat in my life."

Camilo smiled knowingly and stood his ground. "Seester, if the Spirit wants you to be fat, who are we to question?" And as if to get her started, he walked over to the table, turned the bag of fruit upside down, and held up a mango in her direction.

The two of them contentedly munched on fresh fruit and I sat up in bed, feeling much better and calmer. As I watched my two friends eating and giggling like children, I realized that I had been missing the point. I had been so busy trying to understand everything that I had passed over this unusual opportunity to be a child again, to live without questions, to enjoy things that I did not understand and maybe never would. So many of the Filipinos were like children. Perhaps this innocence was what made it possible for them to accept these paranormal realities as if they were nothing more than everyday occurrences. It was the message in my dream. As I observed the innocence of my two beautiful and powerful friends, I felt so fortunate to be in their company.

"You are seeing so many things for the first time," Camilo said. With his mouth full, it was even more challenging to decipher his English. For that matter, with his missing teeth, he would probably be just as hard to understand in his native tongue. "It is all difficult for you to accept. You must give yourself time. The Philippines are a holy land, filled with blessings and miracles. Your body is not yet ready to digest all that you have seen and heard. This is why you had pain in your stomach. You must meditate to become stronger so you can accept all that is available to you. You are here with a good teacher."

He and "Looee" exchanged wet, mango smiles.

"The young boy who spoke last night is a very powerful medium."

I was tickled because he pronounced the word as if it were spelled *meejum*.

"He started channeling when he was three years old. His message last night was about you, Seester Andrea. He said that you have spent other lifetimes here in the Philippines. One day you will also be a *meejum* and you will remember your past lives here. You have returned to continue your studies which began at another time. You will be spending much time here in the future, learning about healing and the Philippine mysteries. You will be an instrument in teaching what you have learned in many other parts of the world and enlightening the people with the truth."

My mouth fell open in surprise.

Camilo looked closely at Lois and me, studying our faces. "I see beautiful colors in your auras. You could both be *meejums*. But you have not yet developed these powers. You must make your nervous systems very strong so you can allow your spirit guides to speak through you. Ask them to come to you. We in the Philippines have a tradition of *meejumship*. Many of our parents are already channels for spirit and we have been trained at a very young age to communicate with Spirit. It is not unusual to us.

"It is different with you. Because of your nonspiritual society, *meejumship* is confusing. You became sick because you were fighting a battle. You wanted to digest these new ideas, but your mind was fighting to stay connected to the old ones. Perhaps the Spirit was trying to enter you, Seester, but your ego did not want to give up control."

Mango juice was dripping down his chin and he wiped it with his shirtsleeve before he continued. "There is much to learn about Spiritism. We continue to study and practice all the time because the spirits give us guidance and help us with our spiritual mission here on earth. They show us the way to accept each other and to lose our fear of the life-death cycle of the material world. In the physical, we are separate, but in spirit, we are all one. When we are truly able to see ourselves in each other, then we can create a loving world and inspire others to do the same."

I felt the truth in his words. Ever since I had arrived, my stomach and digestion had been a problem. Alex had helped me momentarily, but my attachment to the old ways had invited the trouble to return. Now too much had happened for me to hold on to the past. I was tunneling into the future at an astoundingly rapid pace and there was no turning back.

I did not know what to make of the boy's message. It all seemed so impossible, but apparently he had said it and something inside of me had heard him. I had no idea what to expect but I felt that I had become young enough to appreciate whatever adventures were in store. I turned back to my two playmates, determined to leave the old world behind.

7

ECHOES
OF THE
PAST

Deep in the interior of the Philippine island of Luzon, there rests a large, richly fertile province called Pangasinan, reputed to be the region where psychic surgery originated. Although many have emigrated to other areas, most of the practicing psychic surgeons were either born in Pangasinan or have ancestors who originated there. It is an expansive land of rice and sugarcane farms, and the natives are seriously involved in superstition and ritual.

Lois and I were on our way to visit this legendary province. Our bus was clipping along at a speed well above the safety zone, and as usual, I was holding on to the seat in front of me, hoping that I would live to see the other end of the journey. Lois stopped a sweet-looking girl walking down the aisle, the hostess on this land flight, and asked her how long the trip would take.

She smiled graciously and answered in a high-pitched, strongly accented lilt, "We will be traveling for about four to five hours, Mum."

"Last year, it only took about three and a half," Lois commented to me.

The hostess, overhearing her, informed us with the same smile never leaving her face, "Yes, mum, it used to take three and a half hours, but last week we killed ten Canadians, so the driver has slowed down. Have a nice trip, mum, and let me know if there is anything I can do to make you more comfortable."

She calmly walked on down the aisle and Lois looked at me, shrugged her shoulders, and dropped her head down into her newspaper. Feeling exceedingly vulnerable, my mind began to complain like a Jewish grandmother. If the operations didn't get you, the driving would. I shifted nervously in my seat, wondering what the odds were of returning home alive.

I looked around the bus at all the Filipinos who were either dozing or staring casually out the windows. No one else seemed concerned in the slightest, so I shifted my attention to the beautiful farmlands that we were sailing past. It seemed that the deeper we moved into the countryside, the worse the roads became, until the driver was forced to slow down to a speed that was almost tolerable. I managed to stop fearing for my life and involved myself with the scenery around me. The rice fields were carefully roped off, clearly defining the boundaries between properties. The workers were out in the fields in their colorful straw hats, trudging through the mud and irrigation ditches. The richer ones pulled large water buffalo, their living tractors, by the huge rings through their noses, urging them through the fields in the hot sun. Owning a water buffalo was a sign of prestige, and in many places along the way, I saw farmers tenderly hand-washing these massive animals.

Now more than ever, as we moved further into the countryside, everything that I looked upon was unfamiliar, and so were my most recent memories. It felt as if I had entered a new planet where language, sounds, and even the smells were foreign. At this point, I had gone beyond doubts and fears. The whole thing was simply undecipherable. My mind was like an old computer that needed to be updated in order to utilize the new input. I relaxed, somehow taking comfort in knowing that since there was no way to process the information, I was no longer responsible.

We traveled along without incident for several hours until the bus pulled up to make a short pit stop at a small roadside restaurant called Hungry Tummy. Mine wasn't, due to the fact that I was still a bit sensitive from the operation the day before, and the hot newsflash about the ten Canadians had done nothing for my digestion. I sipped some tea and relaxed on terra firma for a while until we climbed back on the bus to resume our journey to the interior of this ancient world.

It was midafternoon when we pulled up and stopped in front of the Urduja Hotel. It was located on the main street of a very small commerical town called Urdaneta. We left the bus, grabbed our bags, and carried them inside the rather sinister lobby, stopping at the registration desk. The air, denser and staler than it had been in Manila, seemed to hang like a thick cloud of old memories. Lois had stayed here before and the young clerk remembered her. She greeted us warmly, yelling to the bellboy, asleep in the corner, to carry our bags upstairs.

"Excuse me," Lois said. "Could we please have a room on the other side of the hotel so that it will not be noisy?"

"Of course, mum," she agreed.

She changed our key for another and we followed the sleepy bellboy upstairs. He let us in to a very dark, stuffy room, with two tiny beds and three wastebaskets. I wondered what we would have to throw away. The bellboy ambled over to the window and turned on the much-needed air conditioner, which spouted and puffed for a while until it settled into a long, continuous noisy wheeze of cool air. We gave him a tip which he accepted through half-closed eyelids and left.

While we unpacked our things, Lois told me about her previous stay here. "This hotel was built next to a slaughterhouse. The reason I asked for a special room is because last year, I was awakened in the middle of the night by the screams of animals being slaughtered. I was unable to sleep as it went on most of the night and I felt terribly upset when I awakened in the morning. I tried to transfer to another hotel, but apparently this is the only one in town. It won't happen this time because we are on the other side, away from the slaughterhouse. Besides," she added with a smile, "that air conditioner would drown out the Third World War."

We relaxed until dinnertime, while she told me about David Oligani, the healer that we would be visiting the next day. She said that here, in the interior of the Philippines, there was a great deal of ignorance and superstition among the communities. Black witchcraft was a common practice, with people trying to take control over others by mental manipulation. Victims of these manipulations often felt ill and manifested physical body ailments that were undetectable by doctors. David, as well as being a psychic surgeon, had a particular specialty that she had found fascinating. He was able to detect these subtle negative energies inflicted by means of witchcraft spells and remove them from people's bodies. I couldn't imagine what that would look like but I knew I would find out soon enough.

We had an early dinner and prepared for sleep. I was exceptionally tired—in fact, I had felt that way ever since we arrived at this hotel. I thought it must be from the long journey and I was glad to settle in to my bed. But as tired as I was, it took me a long time to fall asleep.

The sound started while I was still in a dream, but it pulled me sharply back to reality. My eyelids felt as heavy as water buffalo. When I managed to pry them open, I looked around the dark room listening to the screams, feeling trapped in a world of death and horror. It was the animals. They were being slaughtered next door and I could not detach from their shouts of pain and fear. Suddenly they stopped, and all I could hear was the drone of the air conditioner, echoing their yells in my ears. I looked over at Lois to see if she had heard them. She appeared to be sound asleep. I thought the clerk had assigned us a room away from this nighttime terror, but apparently, the girl had misunderstood. I lay back down, dead tired, but somehow not wanting to go back to sleep. I heard Lois stir, fitfully turning over in her tiny bed. The sounds were gone, but something must have been troubling her also. We said nothing to each other, just lay there in the dark until I finally drifted into a light sleep, afraid to go too deep.

About an hour later, it happened again. This time I was awake immediately, praying for a way to block my ears against this horrifying sound of animal mass murder. Again, it only lasted a few moments. The air conditioner reclaimed my attention and I wondered how these terrifying screams had so clearly made it through the loud drone of that noisy machine. I drifted back into a half-sleep state.

I spent the rest of the night in a troubled daze, continuously violated by the nightmarish sounds going on outside the window. I seemed to keep awakening an instant before the screams began and by the time I was fully conscious, they would stop. When morning arrived, I felt as if I had had no sleep at all. Lois also looked tired and irritable, and we sat up in bed, just staring at each other.

I finally broke the silence. "Did you hear it?"

"Yes, I heard it all night long, but each time I looked over at you, I thought you were out. I didn't want to say anything, in case you were lucky enough to be sleeping through it."

I stumbled out of bed, and flipped off the air conditioner. My ears were ringing and I opened the window to get some fresh air. As early as it was, the heat was already quite intense, and our room filled with the dense humidity. Although we broke out into a sweat, it was a relief to stop the machine noise and let in some new energy from the sun. We quickly showered and went downstairs.

We headed straight for the reception desk and rang for the clerk. She lazily shuffled up to the desk in her rubber clogs and looked at us questioningly.

"Yes, mums? Can I help you?" she inquired.

"Yes, dear," Lois said. "When we checked in, I asked if you

could give us a room on the other side, away from the slaughter-house. We were up all night listening to the screams. We need to change our room."

The little clerk stared at Lois for a full minute before she started giggling hysterically. I was furious! Had she placed us there purposely so that we would be terrorized? She finally stopped laughing, looked at us both, and said, "But, mums, that slaughterhouse is empty. They built a new one just outside of town. This one has not been in use for over eight months." She shuffled away, giggling to herself, probably pleased that she had a great piece of gossip for her friends about the crazy Americans who had just checked in and were hearing things.

Lois and I staggered into the coffee shop and ate our breakfast in complete silence. We did not know what to say to each other. But we both knew what we had heard, and that the echoes of past actions keep calling to the present.

We finished eating and walked outside to find some transportation to take us to our next destination: David Oligani, the witch detective.

8

WORLD
OF WITCHES

Lois and I must have been quite a sight with our long American legs tucked snugly beneath us in the side cab of a tricycle, hair flowing in the breeze. We were utilizing the most popular mode of transportation in Urdaneta, the tricycle pedicab.

Our driver was delighted that we had chosen him; he maintained a huge grin during the entire ride, pedalling us dutifully over the torn-up roads toward our destination. Very few Americans venture into this backroads part of the Philippines, so we attracted a great deal of attention as we passed. Everyone who saw us broke into enormous smiles, pointing and shouting greetings. The children were shocked and then excited, running beside the tricycle as far as their legs would carry them. Between the blond hair, blue eyes, and white skin, we were some kind of living movie fantasy that had come to visit their world, and they were thrilled.

After bumping along for about twenty minutes, we pulled up in front of a small farmhouse. We handed the driver a few extra coins, and he was ecstatic. Even when we told him we might be here for hours, he wanted to wait to drive us back at no extra charge. He lit up a cigarette, leaned against his tricycle and stared out into the farmlands, as patient as the coconut trees surrounding him.

The wooden door to the farmhouse opened and out came a short, gray-haired middle-aged woman to see who had arrived at her front gate. When she spotted Lois, she rushed over to her and energetically hugged her.

"Mary!" Lois hugged her back. "How are you? I am so happy to see you again. This is my companion, Andrea. Is David here?"

"Yes. He is in the house. You follow me," she answered, eyeing me curiously. Not letting go of Lois's hand, she led her into the house. I followed behind, reflecting that Mary was a popular name in this very Catholic country.

The front door opened into a large, nearly empty wooden room, with folding chairs placed along the outer walls. Directly ahead, a checkered curtain closed off the busy kitchen. It seemed that there was always food cooking in Philippine kitchens, with no particular regard for mealtimes. In the middle of the living room was a long staircase that led to the upper quarters, cluttered with reclining cats and dogs of various shapes and sizes.

Mary sat us down and, stepping over the sleeping animals, ran upstairs to tell her husband that we had arrived. We were lucky that he was at home—they had no telephone, and there had been no way to forewarn them. She came running back down the stairs shouting orders into the kitchen. Pulling the curtain back to greet us, three of their daughters emerged. They brought out a table on wheels bearing coffee, tea, and fresh papaya and pineapple. Mary let us know with great pride that this fruit had come from her own trees. We drank tea and chatted, munching on the ripe, succulent fruit. Mary told us that there had been some patients from Switzerland visiting that morning, and now David was resting. In a few moments, a very short, dark, smiling man wearing glasses and a T-shirt with multiple tears in it walked down the stairs, climbing through the jungle of animals who were not the slightest bit interested in moving. He walked gently up to Lois and pressed his cheek to hers.

"Welcome to the Philippines, Seester. I am so happy that you are here in my country once again." His voice was soft and sweet, slightly high-pitched and very peaceful.

Lois introduced us and he shyly shook hands with me. He seemed so meek and retiring, it was difficult to imagine that he could ever have the power to battle with black witches and dark energy. Lois asked him if he would mind working this afternoon and he seemed surprised that she would have any doubts. Of course, he would work. He just needed to change his shirt and we could go into the chapel. In fact, he said, there were already some people there waiting for him. As he rose to change, I noticed that three fingers on his left hand were missing down to the knuckle. I wondered how a psychic surgeon could work with only one good hand.

He disappeared upstairs only to return a few minutes later in his formal wear for operating, a T-shirt identical to the one he had removed, only this one had just one hole in it. He motioned for us to follow him out the door to the small chapel standing beside the house. Mary, shouting orders to her daughters, grabbed a fan and took up the rear.

From the moment I entered it, I fell in love with David's chapel. Rows of benches filled the space that led up to the raised platform that served as both altar and healing room. A massage table stood in the center of the platform, and a masterful hand-painted mural completely covered the wall behind it. In soft pastel colors, the mural displayed a path, surrounded by trees, leading to small mountains lining the horizon. Showers of golden and white rays of light burst open and poured down from the heavens. Purple clouds were scattered throughout the light, which floated beneath a huge all-seeing eye. Just below the eye was a symbolic dove flying downward, bringing the divine healing energy to the earth. Angels, blowing trumpets and floating in a rich blue sky, bordered the uppermost portion, creating a feeling of celebration and protection.

A small group of Philippine women were already in the chapel, napping on the hard benches, using pages of newspaper as pillows. When we arrived, they sat up and came forward to stand on the sides of the raised platform. David stood behind his table and led a short prayer, thanking God for our safety and for bringing us all together. Mary sat on a bench off to the side of the table, staring directly at us with tremendous interest and focus, wildly fanning away the mosquitoes and burping loudly at intervals. She laughed out loud occasionally as she slapped at a bug with the side of her fan, completely oblivious to the fact that she could possibly be disturbing anyone's concentration.

David removed his glasses, laid them on the table, and looked at us.

Lois stepped forward. "I have brought my friend Andrea here to meet you and to show her your spiritual healing. We would like very much to watch you work."

David smiled sweetly and nodded in acknowledgment. "I am very happy to have you here. You have come a very long way. Is there something I can do for you?"

"Well, I have a calcium deposit in my hip, David. Could you remove it for me?" Lois asked.

"I will look," he said. "Please lie down."

Mary rose automatically, dropped her fan and went to his side, swiftly moving his glasses to safety so that no one would lie down on them. She reached into a drawer in the table and brought out cotton, a bowl, holy oil, an empty glass, and matches. Lois pulled down her slacks and reclined on her stomach. He stood and looked intently at her body for a moment, and then raised his right hand, his index finger six inches away, and pointed it at her hip.

I thought he must have been measuring something and waited for him to place his hands on her body to penetrate the skin. But he had something else in mind. He moved his index

finger twice in a short, slicing motion as if he were drawing a
line in the air above Lois's hip. When he dropped his hand, we
all bent over to look. A tiny pink incision had miraculously
appeared on the skin. It was as if he had used a laser on her
from half a foot away. He moved his face closer and closer to
the incision, squinting his eyes as if he were having trouble
seeing it.

"Where is it?" he asked innocently.

Mary impatiently handed him his glasses. "It's right there,"
she said pointing with a patronizing annoyance in her voice.
"Put on your glasses." She stared at my eyes, caught my amazement, and threw her head back, cackling with laughter. She
then dipped a piece of cotton in holy oil, and placed it in the
bottom of the glass. Lighting a match, she set the piece of cotton
on fire, quickly handed the glass to David and he smacked the
open end over the tiny incision on Lois's hip. The fire went out
instantly, while the vacuum in the glass created a suction which
raised the skin up into it. He left it on for a few minutes and
Mary picked up the fan, taking on the demanding task of keeping the flies away from the holy oil. The pressure of the vacuum
on the skin caused the incision to separate, allowing blood to
seep out into the glass. We waited for about thirty seconds until,
with a decided yank, David pulled the glass away. With his
good hand, he reached in through the bloody incision and removed a long, stringy substance that looked like the same stuff
Alex had called calcium. A quick wipe of a towel and Lois's
hip was nearly clean. Only the tiny original incision remained,
a reminder of what had just taken place.

"That will disappear in a few days," he reassured us.

Lois stood up, pulling up her slacks, and thanked him. The
entire process was obviously painless, because Lois's face had
remained placid.

David smiled at me and nodded as if to say, "The operation
was a success."

I used the eye contact as an opportunity to speak with him.
I wanted to know if he diagnosed in the same way that Alex

did. "How did you know where the problem was? Could you see it?" I asked.

"When I look into the aura, sometimes I see a red flower. That tells me where the trouble is located." He thought for a moment. "Sometimes I hear a voice. Sometimes I just know." He shrugged his shoulders and walked away to join some of the people who had been there watching.

I went to sit on a bench until the next treatment. I thought about what a sweet spirit he must have if illness appeared to him as a flower. Mary had the table cleaned up and cleared off in about two minutes without missing a beat in her insect shooing duty. Then she sat beside me, swatted a few of her adversaries away from my legs, and burped. She had a face that looked indomitable. I could tell that she was the matriarch of this establishment, that she was the one who kept things going.

She smacked her fan on my leg and pointed over to David. She wanted me to watch him. I obeyed. He was in a conversation with a sweet and shy-looking old woman in a ragged blue print dress. He listened to her, nodding his head. They seemed to have an excellent rapport. Gently taking her hand, he led her to the table, inviting her to lie down on her back. He began to look around as if he were missing something. He was like an absent-minded professor, the type who could easily spend an entire day looking for the eyeglasses that were resting on the top of his head. Mary was quickly at attention by his side. Opening the drawer in the table, she pulled out a towel and placed it in his hands. She was completely devoted to him, keeping track of all the little details. They made a bizarre and wonderful team.

David tenderly stroked the forehead of the old woman and looked at us.

"She has not been feeling well. I think she has a witch, so I will test her. If you hear a loud wail, it is the voice of the witch," he informed us.

I was almost afraid to listen or to see any more. But my curiosity overwhelmed my fear. All the women gathered closely round to watch while he walked to her feet at the end of the table. Placing the towel over her toes, he raised that famous index finger to his mouth and blew sharply on it. He immediately placed the tip of the finger on the towel over a particular spot on her big toe. He applied a small amount of pressure, his gaze glued to her face. The woman grimaced, obviously feeling some pain. David removed his finger and blew on it once again, then reapplied it to the same area on her toe. He slowly and steadily applied more and more pressure until the woman cried out. With one last blow, he pressed into her toe with force. The woman let out a loud, shrill shriek which promptly turned into a unmistakable wail of distress. I shrunk back toward the corner of the room, frightened for the woman and for myself.

David smiled triumphantly and, maintaining the intense pressure on the toe, he called out in a high sing-songy voice, "Welcome to the Philippines." He was talking to the witch. His voice changed suddenly, becoming deep and foreboding. "Get out or I will burn you out!" he commanded.

He turned to us and said quietly, "She is a female witch and she is very stubborn." He helped the woman sit up and began to smack her on the thigh, continuously hitting her harder and harder. Each time she was hit, the poor old woman wailed like a demon in a horror movie and Mary laughed. David saw my dismay at what he was doing and stopped for a moment, looked compassionately at me, and said, "Don't worry. This is my auntie." I guess a wave of relief was supposed to wash over me with that information.

The observers had formed a half-circle around the platform and David forcefully took the old woman by the hand. He proceeded to make the rounds with her, stopping at each person. She took each individual's hand in hers and placed it momentarily at her forehead in a gesture that appeared to be reverent. When she got to Lois and me, we offered our hands and David looked pleased. "I am allowing the witch to ask forgiveness for her deeds. I am giving her the opportunity to repent for her soul before I send her out from my auntie's body."

When they had finished, he laid her back on the table. The air felt terribly dense and I wondered how much longer this could continue. David studied the old woman's face for a moment and then reached for the towel, placing it over her toe once again. He stood with his eyes closed, breathing, and he appeared to be gathering a great deal of internal energy. The room was still. With a definitive gesture, he blew hard on his finger and, moving in slow motion, placed it carefully back on the toe. His aunt was silent. As he began to apply pressure, I could feel a vortex of energy building around him, pulling everything toward it with great force. I had to hold on to my seat because I felt as if I were being drawn into a whirlwind. One more shot of pressure on the toe and the silence was broken as the old woman let loose with a wail and Mary let out a loud fart.

The rest of us had moved back into the corners of the room, attempting to escape the force of the witch. I huddled close to Lois. The wailing continued for several moments, diminishing in intensity until gradually it stopped. Inhuman heavy breathing took its place, sending chills up and down my spine. And then it was over. "Bye-bye," David called out sweetly, as we followed the witch's invisible flight with our eyes.

The sudden stillness that followed transported me back to a time in my childhood when my family and I had confined ourselves to our cottage during a furious hurricane in Nantasket Beach. When it was over, we had walked outside and it had felt like this, as if the whole world were purged and renewed. I breathed deeply and relaxed my body, noticing that I had been holding my breath. We all slowly crept out of the corners of the room and walked toward the old woman lying quietly on the table.

Tears were gathered in the corners of her eyes and she was gently breathing and praying. David ran his hands up and down the center of her body, stopping at her stomach, solar plexus, heart and her spiritual third eye located in the middle of her forehead. Blessing her with the sign of the cross, he tenderly whispered to her in Tagalog and she quietly and respectfully answered.

David kissed his aunt on the forehead and motioned for her to get up. She turned to her friends with a smile on her face. Mary stepped forward holding a bottle containing some strange type of herbal mixture floating in oil and gave it to the old woman, who thanked her and went to sit on a bench by the side of the room. David sat back down, dropped his head in prayer and then left the chapel. Mary grabbed me by the hand.

"You come with me to the house. We will eat now," she directed.

Eating was the last thing I wanted to do, but I had been well-trained by now and I followed her orders. We passed our pedicab driver, who was smoking and listening to some seventies rock-and-roll music on a portable radio. He flashed us a smile, serenely patient and perfectly happy to be doing nothing.

When we got to the house, Mary's daughters had laid out a huge spread of food, fresh from the farm. Lois winked at me and we dug in.

"My father is a very spiritual man," David told us while we ate. "Sometimes he is talking away to the air and everyone thinks he is crazy. But he isn't. He talks to the spirits. He looks into the ground and he can see the water flowing under the earth. Sometimes he is crying because a spirit told him something sad."

He pushed back from the table. "It was little bit difficult to catch the witch in my auntie because she was hiding. Very sneaky!" He snickered. "When I finally caught her, she was wailing because she was angry that I found her. I made her tell everything that she had done. I had complete control over her. I could have made her dance. But all I wanted was to lift her consciousness so that she may evolve into the light. I did not hurt my auntie. I only hurt the witch, because that was the only way I could make her listen. You know, there are twenty-nine kinds of sickness caused by witches. They must be found and disciplined.

"My auntie is a good woman but she is spiritually weak.

That is how the witch was able to hurt her. I blessed her and gave her herbs in oil to rub on her body to strengthen her, but if her faith does not become stronger, the witch will come back." He shook his head in sadness. "I will pray for her. Now I will rest. Thank you for coming to my house."

I didn't want to leave. I adored this sweet man and I could have listened to him talk all day. We hugged and I watched him climb the stairs until he was out of sight.

Mary wrapped some papaya in a napkin and handed it to us for the ride home. She walked us outside and kissed us good-bye. "You come back to see me again," she instructed. I knew that some day I would follow these parting orders.

9

ASSISTANT

The wild bus ride back seemed uneventful compared to what had happened in Pangasinan. When the black, choking diesel fumes poured in the windows, I knew we had arrived in the heart of Manila. We spent the day relaxing and swimming in the pool at the hotel, resting up from our visit to the province. There was so much to assimilate.

We rose early the next morning, arriving at Alex's center before the healing session began. When I passed through the orange gate and saw the assistants congregated on the benches, administering to the hordes of sick people, I knew that something had shifted. Since my journey to the interior, the old feelings of awe and disbelief had passed. I now felt at home and eager for whatever new experiences might be coming my way. Even the attitudes of Alex's assistants were different. They greeted me familiarly, as if it were the most natural thing in the world for me to be there.

I scanned the area and felt attracted to a petite, well-dressed

Philippine woman who was holding a very young child. I sat beside them, affectionately rumpling the little girl's hair.

"Is she well?" I asked her mother.

"Oh, yes," she replied emphatically. "She is fine, now. Reverend Orbito saved her life. She had a brain tumor and the doctors said she would die in three months." Her eyes filled up with tears. "I didn't know what to do. Then a friend asked me if I had brought her to a faith healer. I didn't believe in such things but I was desperate. I had heard that Reverend Orbito was supposed to be one of the best, so I asked my husband what he thought. He became very angry and told me not to come here, but I came in secret after he went to work. After about six sessions, she was completely healed. The doctors couldn't believe it and neither could my husband. He came to meet the Reverend and thank him. That was already two years ago. Now, I bring her back sometimes for a check-up, but she is always fine."

I gave the woman a hug and congratulated her for her courage. The little girl had wandered away while we were talking and was happily sucking on an old discarded piece of candy she had picked up from the ground.

"Excuse me," the mother called and ran to rescue her baby.

I walked on.

A man with a jaw that was swollen out about four inches was being treated by a young magnetic healer* called Sister Mercy. She was quite frail and attractive, and she smiled sweetly when she saw me, motioning for me to come and pray with her. I sat beside her and watched her travel deeper and deeper inside herself until she had moved into a full trance. Standing majestically, she placed her hands on the man's jaw. All at once, her face contorted dramatically, her hands became rigid, and she began to utter some incomprehensible sounds. Her right

---

*Magnetic healing is a form of faith healing which does not involve penetration of the skin or the materialization of diseased tissue. The healer simply draws in the magnetic energy naturally present in the atmosphere and sends it out through the hands into the patient's body.

hand took a shape as if she were holding a hypodermic needle. After hesitating a moment to focus her concentration, she brought her hand to a particular spot on the man's jaw. Slowly, her thumb pressed the end of the invisible syringe while, to my astonishment, the skin indented slightly as if it were actually being punctured by the needle that wasn't there. The man remained perfectly still and prayed while she pressed her fingers into the swollen area on his face. Some white, foul-smelling liquid oozed out. She wiped it off and did it again. This went on for about ten minutes until her fingers relaxed, her face returned to normal, and she quieted down. She placed her hands on the top of his head for a final prayer and sat. She was peaceful and attractive as before, with no sign that she had just looked like a demon-possessed character in a horror film.

"He had an abscessed tooth that became badly infected," she explained. "The doctors can do nothing for him until we remove the infection. I have been giving him psychic injections and he has done very well. His jaw has gone down about two inches in the last two weeks. Come and do magnetic healing with me."

She showed me how to place my hands to clear away the negativity and to tune in to the electromagnetic force fields of energy already present in the atmosphere. I watched her open her hands toward the sky, draw in this energy, and then infuse it into his jaw. I copied her movements and we worked together for a few minutes. I didn't really feel anything but I thanked her for the instruction and as I prepared to walk away, the man timidly touched my hand and said, "God bless you." I was moved by his innocence and wanted to set him straight that he was thanking the wrong person, that I had really done nothing. But I didn't want to hurt his feelings by being ungrateful, so I left it as it was.

Wandering toward a bench at the front of the room, I saw one of the women healers examining a large protrusion on the chin of a baby. She laid the baby down, asked for a bowl and some water and prayed for a moment, obviously setting her intention and asking the spirit for help in the healing. To my disgust, she then placed her mouth around the swelling and began to breath in, making short sucking sounds. Every few minutes, she would lift her head, spit some whitish liquid into the bowl, rinse out her mouth, and do it again. It seemed like it must be a terrible ordeal for her, but she appeared to be easy with the process. The baby's mother was looking on unemotionally, as if she had seen this many times before.

When the healer was through, she rubbed the baby's chin with holy oil and moved on to another patient. I asked the mother what was wrong with her child. She said she didn't really know. The baby had been born with this deformity, and at certain times, it swelled. When the infection was sucked out, it would return to its normal size. I told her I hoped her child would grow up to be healthy and strong.

The sound of a woman moaning in delirium drew me to where a crowd was gathered. Several healers were praying over this woman and every time she moaned, one of them would yell something in a commanding voice. Then the woman would moan again. I saw Mary, Alex's first assistant, standing by her side and I made my way in to stand beside her.

"What is her problem?" I asked. "Why are they yelling at her?"

"They are not yelling at her. She has a bad spirit," she told me. "They are trying to frighten this bad one and ask the good spirits to heal her. She wants to cooperate, but the bad spirit is strong. We need very much light to help us. You join and pray. Send light to the woman for she is a good woman. She just got confused by too much negative thinking. Now, she has forgotten how to be positive and she has become weak."

I looked at this poor raving woman and I prayed for her, comparing her situation with that of David Oligani's aunt. I thought that only David worked with this kind of negativity, because I hadn't yet seen it anywhere else. Although they didn't call it a witch here and the treatment was far less dramatic, it was certainly the same thing; someone falling so deeply into the habit of negative thinking, there was no alternative besides outside intervention. Her moaning began to taper off and it looked as if she were allowing herself to relax a little. A few seconds later, she became conscious and opened her eyes. When she saw the group surrounding her, her eyes filled up with tears and she buried her head in her hands. I walked away, embarrassed for her. Mary followed me and lit up a cigarette.

"Will she be all right now?" I asked.

"Only if she learns how to make her mind strong. At midnight, we pray for all the people that we have healed. You pray for her tonight. Ask for her mind to become strong so that she can become well."

I didn't think that I could be much help but I vowed to try.

"You know," Mary said, "it is up to the patients whether or not they will heal. It is all in the mind. When Alex was in Saudi Arabia last year, a strange thing happened. He went to visit a man who had made a miracle. The man told him that only two years before, he had been almost dead from cancer of the lungs. The doctor was giving him treatment but it did not help. One day, this miracle happened. The X rays showed no cancer at all. He jumped for joy. He began to feel better almost immediately. In a few weeks, his strength came back. In six months, he went back to work and felt fine.

"They found out later that they had made a mistake by confusing his X rays with those of a healthy man. Because he believed he was fine, he became fine. When the other man saw the mistaken bad X rays, his health got bad until he became very sick." She pointed to her head. "It is all in the mind."

Mary snuffed out her cigarette and began to gather all the assistants together. She walked up to Lois and me and said, "Alex wants you both to be assistants today. I will tell you what to do."

I was surprised and delighted. Mary placed Lois at the head of the table, handing her some cotton. She gave me the bowl into which he would be dropping the extracted matter. We began to sing the prayers and Alex entered the room, looking very deep and far away. He gave us a quick nod of recognition and sat in his chair behind the table. I was thrilled and a little scared, hoping that I could fit into this finely tuned machine that performed with perfect precision.

The session went on as before, with Mary standing guard, leading the crowds in and out. Everyone worked with such fastidiousness that Alex never got a spot of blood on his white shirt. Mary showed Lois how to hold her hands so that while she would not be obstructing the view of the observers, the blood would neatly fall into the cotton. I stood by Alex's left side, closely following the motion of his hands with my eyes. When he was ready to remove the material, I was ready with the bowl so that he could effortlessly drop the stuff in without having to search around. I fell into the rhythm of the action, and each time my hands came close to his, I could feel the healing energy moving up my spine until my head was buzzing. I felt as if I were living in a waking dream-state in which I was ultrasensitive to each sound and each person that passed through the room. Just as before, while I was with Alex, all my doubts disintegrated and my mind stopped plaguing me.

Time disappeared and I was fully present as the long line of patients floated through my awareness. I no longer distinguished one personality or sickness from another. I was merely a cog in a wheel, performing my function with ease and precision. Then a young woman who looked about my age was carried in. With the help of several people, she pulled herself painfully up on the table. Mary lifted her blouse and I saw the source of her pain. She must have had breast cancer because the whole upper portion of her chest was swollen and oozing. I was horrified and repelled. Alex turned to diagnose the woman and, making a distorted face, he turned away for a moment, composing himself so that he could continue. I wanted to cry out at the unfairness of it but I controlled myself. The woman had already suffered enough. I had lost my concentration and I looked into Alex's face, searching for some comfort or explanation of why this hideous disease had overtaken an otherwise lovely-looking human being. When his eyes met mine, I felt an electrical charge travel through my body and my wrist jumped, clumsily overturning the bowl and spilling the blood and diseased tissue on the sleeve of Alex's shirt.

"Aah!" he called out in surprise. He raised his eyebrows and flashed a quick shot of anger at me. I was devastated and I wished that the floor would open up and swallow me. Mary rushed to my rescue and efficiently wiped his shirt sleeve until only a slight stain remained. He relaxed and tuned in to my upset. With softened eyes, he looked at me clearly, smiled gently and whispered to me, "Never mind. You forget about that. You are good assistant." His kindness touched me and, still shaking, I returned my concentration to the business at hand. I knew that we would never speak of this, but I saw what could happen when I allowed my emotional involvement to block my concentration. One had to build solidity and steel nerves to take part in Alex's world. The healing continued.

He turned back to the woman, closed his eyes, and allowed his hands to penetrate her chest just to the side of the worst swelling. He removed blood clots and small bits of what looked like cysts. He entered her chest area in three separate places. The smell was repulsive. When he was through, he dipped his fingers in holy oil and made the sign of the cross in the center of her forehead, praying quietly over her. She thanked him with her eyes, and when they carried her back out, part of me went with her. The people kept coming.

I had no idea how much time had passed when Alex finally sat back, deciding to take a break. He cleaned his hands and walked shakily out of the room, heading for his office. Lois and I followed closely behind him and as he disappeared behind the door, he said in a very thin voice, "You just wait."

I sat in the chair outside his office, pulling myself back together, thankful for the time to relax.

The door opened and Alex motioned for us to enter. Looking revived and refreshed, he began to speak.

"So, now you are my assistants." He beamed. "I see that you have the vibrations of a spiritual healer. It is good for you to learn here and take these lessons back to your country. Even here in the Philippines, there are many people who do not believe these things that we do. Many ask for proof, but this is not always easy. They invite doctors and scientists, bring in video cameras and ask us to demonstrate. Sometimes we are successful, but often we cannot perform because the stress is too much. Healing happens as it is needed in the moment. This is why we cannot use our powers to walk through walls or slice through tables. We are given the power to heal, not to entertain. It is difficult to concentrate when people treat us like circus performers or freaks. We are human beings, just like you.

"Sometimes we become discouraged because there are so many fakes who trick people for money and attention. They ruin our reputation. I have a group I call the Faith Healer's Circle. I ask the good healers to join so that we may become stronger and have protection. In this way, if people know we are members of the Circle, they know that they are in good hands."

He paused to inhale deeply on his cigarette. The smoke slowly floated out of his mouth, circling his head like a halo.

He continued. "Even when we do healing, we do not focus on the illness. We focus on the spiritual uplifting of the patient. Sometimes it is too late for the physical body to survive. But if the spirit has been uplifted, even if the patient dies, the treatment was a great success. If it is the karma* of that person to die, we cannot interfere. We can only help to change the karma through spiritual awareness.

"This is difficult for your Western world. Many of you believe that there is only one life and when it is finished, we

---

Karma is an Eastern concept based on the laws of cause and effect and reincarnation. Hinduism and Buddhism teach that the quality of a person's life is a direct result of that which occurred in the previous lifetime. If a person was hurtful to others and remained ignorant and unrepenting, he or she must experience the same pain in that life or another, to create a balance and hopefully to learn. Likewise, if the person was benevolent, he or she would have earned a lifetime filled with that same benevolence. It is often believed that awareness of past transgressions can release one from the need to experience that same pain.

are also finished. Here we believe that our spirit returns many times. So, it is our obligation to spiritually enlighten the people."

Lois spoke up. "Alex, I have been watching you work for a long time now. Andrea and I want very much to learn to do psychic surgery. Can you begin to teach us while we are here?"

Alex smiled at Lois and paused to think, gently stroking his own face. "Yah," he said. "I understand you would like to learn to do these material operations but I do not teach this. It takes too much time and prayer and concentration. I have so many people to see. Maybe it is better for you to learn to do magnetic healing. Some of my assistants can teach you and then you can help the people in America."

He rose and gently touched his cheek to mine, saying, "I must talk to the others now. We are all on a mission to spread the spiritual vibration, the medicine that will stop the disease of the Third World War. We are now in the time of the Spirit. Because the Spirit is invisible, if we do not become unified, the world will surely disappear."

We left his room, passing a group of Swedish students who were next in line to speak with him. Outside his office, there were large numbers of foreigners milling around, holding their cameras and their heads, and looking as shocked as I had on the first day I had seen this amazing display of power. They were all asking each other questions that no one knew the answers to. And yet they kept asking. How could the average person integrate this into an otherwise normal life? How could any of us go home and tell our friends that we had just had an operation without anesthesia, without pain, and without recovery time? In most cases it was impossible.

Suddenly, a young Englishman walked over to me and said, "Hello. I saw you assisting, so you must know Reverend Orbito quite well. How does he do it? I just can't understand."

I hesitated. I didn't know any more than he did and he was asking me for help. So I told him what Alex had told me about how he diagnoses and then I explained what Jimmy had said about how the operation is done. The man listened respectfully and seemed greatly relieved by my words. He thanked me and went back to his family to fill them in.

I returned to the benches to relax before the second half began. When I thought about it, I was truly amazed at myself. In my state of awe and bewilderment, I had actually managed to step outside myself to help someone else. I recalled that the young trance channel had said that I would be an instrument in teaching others what I had learned. I had always imagined that before a person could teach something, they had to clearly understand it, but I certainly did not have a clear understanding of psychic surgery. Once again, things were happening differently than I had thought they would.

From my seat, I noticed a few of the magnetic healers gathered around someone who was lying lengthwise across a bench. I approached them more closely, and one of the assistants stepped back to make room for me. There lay the woman with the breast cancer. She fixed her stare on me and I was glued to her, seeing myself in her eyes. As a child, I had sensed that I could make people feel better by placing my hands on them. Although my mind could never grasp it, it was an instinctual knowing that I had always had. Breathing deeply and shutting out the rest of the world, I calmly walked to her side and, joining the others, placed my hands on top of her head as if it were the most natural thing in the world. Flashes of energy shot through my arms while I felt my heart opening, surges of love pulsing through my entire body. I expanded outward and felt myself becoming one with this woman who I knew was nothing more than another manifestation of me. When I opened my eyes, I was perspiring heavily. I was filled with tears and I walked away to be alone, leaving the others to continue their work.

I went into the bathroom and splashed water on my face. I didn't know what had just happened to me, but I had disappeared for a few moments. Perhaps I had gone into a trance. I emerged from the bathroom just in time to see the woman walking slowly on her own power to her friend's car. Something had happened because she no longer needed to be carried.

Whether or not I had had anything to do with it, I wasn't sure. I only knew that she walked.

I found Lois playing with the children and we sat down together to talk.

"What a day!" I said.

Lois nodded her head. "Yes, the energy is very strong. You know, Andrea, I think we need to find someone who will be willing to work with us privately, because I want to learn more. Don't you?"

After what I had just been through, my answer was an unequivocal yes. I thought maybe I would ask Jimmy if he could suggest someone.

We noticed some movement going on in the healing room, but Alex's office door had remained closed. We made our way through the throngs of waiting people and squeezed through the door. The healing had begun, but Alex wasn't doing it.

Behind the table stood a man with huge, deep eyes and a face that reminded me of the alien in *E. T.* He was a little bit taller, rounder and older than Alex, and he worked completely differently. He was flamboyant and excitable and his operations were as wild as Alex's were fastidious. He opened the body with a flourish and the blood flew. It ended up all over his arms, on people's clothing and if we didn't watch out, it landed on our shoes. I watched him, fascinated by the energy in his approach to his work. His eyes were hypnotic and I wondered how he would look when he returned to his normal state of being. He worked on the long line of people with speed and accuracy, appearing to tire more openly than Alex had. When he was finished, he sat down, exhausted, and we left the room. He walked out shortly after us and handed me his business card. It said, Reverend Antonio Romero,* psychic surgeon. His eyes had retained their depth even after he had come out of the trance.

We said good-bye to Alex's assistants, and walked out

*This name has been changed to protect privacy.

through the orange gate to find a taxi. It took a few minutes before a yellow jet came to a screeching halt and we began to climb in. Behind us we heard someone call, "Please wait." It was Antonio. He climbed right in after us, smiling ear to ear.

"I live near your hotel. I would like to accompany you."

"Of course," we said.

Antonio loved to talk. He came from a province in which they interchanged *p*'s with *f*'s, making his thick accent quite interesting and often humorous. I had to listen carefully to understand him, but at least he had all his teeth. He was more than willing to repeat himself if we didn't catch it the first time, which we usually didn't. He quickly filled us in on his family situation. He had a wife and three children and his home was his healing center. He wanted us to come and visit him there.

"Do you teach healing, Tony?" Lois asked him. "We have been here observing for a while and we would like to study. I have been here several times and I'm eager to learn more."

He flashed his eyes at us, looking first at Lois and then at me. "Yes, I teach. In fact, I have an *affrentice* who I taught to do psychic surgery. Do you want to learn to do these material *oferations?*"

I could hardly believe my ears. I never really thought that they could be taught, but at this point, there was nothing that I wanted more.

"Yes. We want very much to learn. How will you teach us?" I wanted to know.

"You come with me now. I will consult the Holy Spirit and if He gives me *fermission*, I will test you to see if you can learn."

He told the taxi driver where he lived. We were now on our way to Tony's home to consult with a spirit for permission to be taught to penetrate human flesh with our bare hands. It was an average day in Manila.

10

TESTING

Tony's house was located just beside the marketplace on a malodorous side street that looked and smelled more like a back alley. The paved road was so narrow that the taxi just barely fit. I have no idea what would have happened if something had been coming in the opposite direction. We paid the driver and Tony led us down a tiny walkway between two of the wooden structures. We stepped over chickens strutting, children playing, and adults lying on the ground, snoozing and eating rice cakes. These adults looked delirious, chanting his name, "Tony, Tony," as we walked through. We learned later that they were mostly dope addicts who lived around here and slept in the alley. We stepped across two boards that were covering some potholes in the ground and stopped at a doorway. Tony rang the bell and amid a chorus of loud barks, a bouncy, smiling woman clamored down the rickety wooden steps to open the locked screen door. She was delighted to see us, graciously inviting us in.

"That's my small lady," he informed us, his interpretation

of "the little woman." Her name was Teresa* and she giggled her way up the stairs, past the excited dogs, and invited us to enter their domicile. We walked into a sunlit room in which every bit of available space was filled with benches, chairs, the customary massage table, a large wooden clock, a TV, and all kinds of wooden religious miniatures and odds and ends. Every inch of the house was covered with something, including the walls, which were plastered with family photos of Tony, Teresa, and their three children. Tony was obviously a family man.

We were standing in a room that tripled as living room, dining room, and healing room. To the left, there was a curtained-off area that served as bedrooms for the entire family, and to the right, yet another curtain hid the kitchen.

Tony gave Teresa a few words of explanation about what we were doing there and she immediately went into the kitchen to prepare a snack. I was becoming accustomed to eating whether I was hungry or not, understanding how important it was to accept these offerings. Food was all that many of our hosts had to give and they were so very generous, always serving us first and making the family wait to eat our leftovers.

"You sit down and relax. We will have a special snack before your test." Tony took his place behind the table and lit a cigarette. The atmosphere was dynamic, with the sunlight pouring in through the windows and the clamor of children running around on the street below. The downstairs door squeaked open, slammed shut, and the sound of running footsteps tapped lightly on the stairs. We turned to see a young boy rush into the room and throw his arms around Tony. It was his youngest son, Ramon.* Tony turned him around to face us and he self-consciously dropped his head.

"These are our *seesters* from America. We will make them feel at home," he told the child.

The little boy nodded at us and ran into the bedroom. Tony

*This name has been changed to protect the privacy of the individual.

sighed. "I love my children so much. Sometimes when we are all together and we are having our dinner, I cannot eat because I am so happy that we are all healthy and have plenty of food. Sometimes I cry when I remember that it was different before."

He launched into a long talk about his life and how he began his work as a healer.

"I was born on November 30, 1932, in Pangasinan. At the age of twenty-two, I became *supervisor* in a steel plant. I became sick in my lungs and it turned into TB. It was very bad and I could not work any more. The doctors said that I could not be healed and I thought I would die. My friends told me to go to see a child who was a spiritual healer. I did not believe in faith healing, but I was DESFERATE!

"This child was only nine years old and when she saw me, she said, 'You know how to heal yourself.' I went away and I began to *fray*. I *frayed* and *frayed* for God to help me.

"One night, about a week later, while I was *sleefing* under my mosquito net, I woke up at four in the morning. I *ofened* my eyes and I could see right through the roof. It was *transfarent!* I could see the blue sky and the stars but I was *faralyzed*. I could not move at all.

"Then I saw a light the size of a one-peso piece, but it *disaffeared*. Then I saw it again and it was two times as big. Again, it *disaffeared*."

His eyes grew wider as he continued his story.

"The third time I saw it, it was a very big circle and it moved down so close to me, I was *apraid* it would pass through my mosquito net and burn me. But it did not. It became a beautiful lady, all dressed in white. She said to me, 'Heal yourself, Tony!' Then she *disaffeared* and she did not come back.

"The next morning, I traveled with my family to a nearby province to visit our relatives. I remember it was November 1, 1954. We slept there and in the middle of the night I had to go to the comfort room. The outhouse was at the other side of the cemetery, and while I was passing through, I suddenly stopped because my body would not move. I saw the light again and I was *apraid*. The light turned into the beautiful white lady, and this time she had a scarf covering her face. My whole body was shaking because I thought it was the sign of death.

"I tried to run away from her but every time I took a step, she stood in my way. Finally, we both stopped and I faced her. I saw that she was floating about three feet above the ground. Then, she removed the scarf and I knew that I was looking at the Virgin Mary.

" 'My dear son, you can heal yourself!' she told me.

" 'How can I? I am only an ordinary citizen. I am not educated,' I answered her.

"She said, '*Fray!* Review your life. Ask for understanding of your sins.'

"Then she gave me a little book. She said, '*Ofen* the book. You will see that it is empty. If you *fray,* letters will *affear.* You read these words and you can heal yourself and others if you want to.'

"And she *disaffeared.* But the book stayed with me and I still have it. I began my *frayers* and healing studies. In a very short time, I healed myself of TB."

As if to accentuate the truth of his story, he took a long puff on his cigarette.

"I did magnetic healing until 1964. Then my mother became very sick. She had a blood clot on her heart and she could not breathe. Many people had come to visit because they were sure that she was dying. I cried and cried because I loved my mother very much. I *flaced* my hands on her heart and I heard the voice of the Virgin Mary telling me, 'You can heal her. You can *oferate* on her heart.' I was *apraid* but she said she would help me. I began to do massage and suddenly, my hands entered her heart cavity. I removed the clot. I was very happy because she did not die. She lived for thirty-six more years and died at the age of ninety-six. That is how I started my healing."

Teresa must have been waiting for the story to end, because the moment Tony finished, the kitchen curtain flew open and she wheeled in a sort of TV tray. They had prepared the perfect spiritual snack for psychic surgery testing: ice cream, sweet rolls, and instant coffee with powdered milk and tons of sugar.

"This is the best ice cream in the world," Tony assured us. "Rocky Road! You eat and then we will see."

I understood why this was a spiritual meal: I had to pray that my stomach would digest it. We dug in and he was right. It was the best ice cream in the world. Between the caffeine, the chocolate, and the sugar, in a few minutes we were totally wired and ready for anything.

Giggling all the while, Teresa wheeled the table back into the kitchen and returned to stand by Tony's side, in case he needed anything. He spoke to her in Tagalog and she scurried around the house, returning with two pieces of carbon paper and some stationery. She handed them to Tony and he placed a carbon between two white pieces of paper and set it on the edge of the table.

"Now, we will begin," he said. "I will first ask the Holy Spirit for *fermission* to test you."

He closed his eyes and went into silence. His face relaxed and soon his head dropped forward. I closed my eyes to join him in the meditation but it was almost impossible to concentrate. What if I failed? And more frightening yet, what if I passed?

When Tony emerged, his eyes had become glassy and his face was flushed. "Yah, it's okay. Now you must concentrate very strong and we will see if you can *ofen* the body. Mama first," he said, referring to Lois.

He motioned for her to approach and sit directly opposite him, facing the papers, using the table as a desk. He instructed me to keep my eyes closed and *fray*. I was dying to open my eyes, but I didn't want to ruin anything for Lois, so I did as I was told. I heard Tony give some directions and then there was silence for a few minutes.

"Okay. Now it is the turn of Seester Andrea." I opened my eyes quickly, hoping to catch a glimpse of something, but Lois was returning to her seat, with a slight glimmer of a grin at the edges of her mouth, the "psycho ward" smile glistening in her eyes. She traded places with me and I took the hot seat.

Tony put aside the papers he had used with Lois and put a piece of carbon between two fresh sheets of white paper. He laid them out in front of me and instructed me to place the tip of the index finger of my right hand in the center of the paper.

"Keep your finger there and concentrate," he instructed. He closed his eyes and went silent for a few moments, obviously moving into a deep state of concentration. I felt a little foolish with my hand poised over these papers at the end of a massage table for no apparent reason, but I waited to see what would happen. In a few seconds, Tony raised his own right hand and held it still, about three inches above mine. With his eyes closed, his body began to sway and his hand began to quiver from the intensity of his concentration. Suddenly, my own fingers started to involuntarily shake, and although he never touched me, the energy forced my index finger hard into the paper. The pressure made my finger move down the paper for several inches. This lasted about twenty seconds until he removed his hand. The energy stopped and my fingers relaxed.

"Okay. You go sit down now," he said gently.

I walked back and sat down next to Lois, wondering if there were more to this test or if we had already done it. We sat quietly, like two school girls, avoiding each others eyes, afraid that we might rudely burst out laughing at the insanity of it all. Tony pulled the carbon out and studied the bottom sheets of paper. He looked up at us, broke into a huge grin and reported the results.

"Congratulations!" he exclaimed. "You have passed the test. You can *ofen* the body! I can teach you to do these material *oferations*. You see?" He held up our handiwork. A jagged line about two inches long went vertically down the center of each paper, the carbon copy results of the involuntary movement of our fingers pressing on the top sheet of paper. Because the line was relatively straight and resembled an incision, that was apparently a sign from the Holy Spirit that we had the ability to *ofen* the body.

We looked incredulously at each other. That was supposed to be it. We had been tested and it was absolutely decided that we had the ability and were now qualified to be taught to do psychic surgery. I guess this called for a celebration because Teresa was already wheeling out the TV tray again and pouring us more coffee.

As I took the caffeine into my system, my body heated up and my thoughts went raging out of control. Me, a psychic surgeon? It was beyond anything that I dared hope for. Yet here was Tony telling me that I could do this and he was willing to teach me. Was this a real test or was he just playing a game? I couldn't imagine why he would do such a thing. What would he get from it? He hadn't asked for any money. I realized that my body was shaking, so I put down the coffee and sat back, trying to gather my thoughts together.

Lois looked as calm and collected as ever. She laid down her cup, thanked Teresa for the refreshment and turned to Tony.

"Well, where do we start?" she asked him.

"You relax this weekend and *fray* to the Holy Spirit. Ask Him to help you and I will also *fray* for you. On Monday morning, you go to the *flace* of Alex and watch everything that he does. You watch his fingers and the way that he moves them. Come to me on Monday afternoon, my next healing day. I will start to teach you. Tonight I will come to you in your dreams and work with you." He got a devilish grin on his face. "Don't be angry if I wake you up."

"I will be going to Mount Banahaw tomorrow morning with Jimmy Licauco. Do you know him?" I asked.

"Oh, yes. I know Jimmy. He writes about the healers. He is a good man. Mount Banahaw is a very holy *flace,* a good *flace* to *fray.* I will see you on Monday."

We hugged goodbye and Tony walked us down the stairs, and through the alley. Lois and I flagged down a taxi, climbed in, and flew across the city toward the hotel. I knew that sleep would be impossible with my mind full of bursting visions of exorcisms, operations, and carbon paper tests.

I could hardly grasp the fact that I had passed the test, that I was to be trained to be a psychic surgeon. I wanted it more than anything in the world. This was the same willful stirring I had when I decided to be a ballet dancer, a feeling which both excited and frightened me, because I knew how it moved me when it ripened into full strength. I anticipated the all-encompassing passion of it, the consuming need to conquer and transform anything in its way. I knew there was no turning back now. The obsession had taken a firm hold on me and I would not rest until I saw my hands part the flesh and *disaffear* inside a human body.

11

SPIRIT SONG

I settled back in my seat, relaxing into the steady motion as we traversed the city, on our way to the legendary Mount Banahaw. Jimmy and Boy had picked me up that morning in an army-green Jeep with an elongated open back. There were hard benches on either side that easily accommodated Jimmy, Boy, myself, and the two young maids who would do the cooking and cleaning. Shopping bags filled with groceries and kitchen utensils lay on the Jeep floor. We would be staying overnight in the mountains, so although we were all wearing our typical light clothing, I had brought along some warmer things to change into. Lois had encouraged me to make this trip while she remained in Manila for the weekend, visiting with some of her friends. This was the first time that I would be venturing anywhere without her and I really felt her absence.

I glanced over at Jimmy and Boy, deep in their own thoughts, and then at the maids, dozing quietly, heads resting on each other's shoulders. The driver sat alone in the front, smoking a cigarette and softly humming to himself. I closed my eyes and the movement of the road lulled me into a soft, sleepy state. As I began to drift, a replay of the dream I had had the previous night floated into my awareness. Once again, I saw myself walking slowly and carefully down a passageway that was the rich brown color of the wet, fertile Philippine earth. I was exploring an underground cave that was strangely familiar.

A massive bump in the road interrupted my vision and I opened my eyes to look at the colorful scenes passing by. People were walking arm in arm, casually chatting and selling their wares in the open markets. Each time we stopped at a red light, young boys ran up to the Jeep to sell us newspapers, candy, and chewing gum. They burst into huge, flirtatious smiles when they saw me, teasing and slapping each other on the back, while they tried out their latest American expressions. They delighted me and I returned their ebullient grins. Blind, crippled beggars made their way into the center of traffic, sticking their rough and needy hands in through the windows, and I gladly gave them my spare change. They took whatever they could get and quickly moved on.

After about an hour's drive through the heated city, we took a welcome turn off the main road and the terrain began to gradually transform into that of more wide open spaces. As we entered the countryside, the breezes, smells, and landscape changed. I watched rice fields and water buffalo appear, much appreciated sights after the chaos and closeness of the crowded streets of Manila. I entered into a reverie about my time with Tony. Perhaps this was the very thing that I had been looking for, the meaning that had been missing from my life. Perhaps I now knew why I had dropped everything and traveled halfway across the world. It seemed such a worthy existence: to heal people. I felt almost drunk with the prospect of returning home as a psychic surgeon. How could I feel anything but good about myself and my life if I could accomplish this feat?

At the next turn, I could feel something provocative in the air, a kind of captivating quality. It was as if the jeep were no longer riding on its own power, as if it had hooked into a tractor beam that was pulling us along. Light was emanating not only from the sky but from the Earth herself, making the thick vegetation look phosphorescent.

As we continued our ride over the pitted roads, we passed native huts made from the palm leaves called *nipa,* roughly constructed, open on all four sides and standing on stilts in order to survive the devastating rains that were unleashed upon the earth every summer. Boy leaned forward and I looked into his sparkling brown eyes. He was about five foot four with a smiling round face. I enjoyed listening to his fluid voice, his nearly perfect English very gently accented. I watched his head bob up and down with the relentless motion of the jeep as he spoke.

"There are more than sixty spiritual and religious groups that maintain houses at the foothills of this mountain. Most of them feel that they are here to reach enlightenment through sacrifice and suffering. There are even some who practice voluntary self-flagellation. My friends and I do not go along with these ways of worship but we all have a common respect for each other's freedom of choice and we manage to live in harmony. We all share acknowledgment of the sacredness of the mountain and the opportunities it affords to open oneself and attune to the higher forces of power that are inherent here. With true power at one's disposal, the challenges and the possibilities are limitless. But before we enter into a relationship with power and accept its offerings, we must understand its true nature and what it will ask of us in return."

Now the mountain itself became visible for the first time. It was gracefully poised against the sky, about 7,000 feet high, they told me. Misty, circular cloud formations hid the uppermost tip from view, as if they had been willed there to hide great mysteries from overly curious and intrusive eyes. I had seen photographs of similar cloud formations around the tip of Mount Shasta, and I wondered if there was a connection.

Boy turned to me on cue and asked, "Have you been to Mount Shasta? She is a sister to our holy mountain. The tip of both mountains are seldom in clear sight. Some associate this particular circular cloud patterning with UFO activity."

I was about to ask for more information when something came into view that stole my attention. Standing directly beside this breathtaking mountain was yet another one, a little bit smaller, but almost exactly like it. I blinked once or twice to make sure that I was not hallucinating but there they stood, side by side. On closer investigation, I could see that there were some marked differences between the two. The tip of the twin was not obstructed with clouds. It could be seen quite clearly and yet it looked darker than the other. It seemed to suggest a general lack of clarity and was as uninviting as Mount Banahaw was compelling.

"That is Mount Kristobal," said Boy. "It is the shadow mountain to Mount Banahaw, the polar opposite, the home of the dark forces. Mount Banahaw offers us a rich spirit world, alive with reflective pools of water, colorful materializations, and clairvoyant and clairaudient occurrences. But she has little to benefit the material planes, as most of her teachings are of a spiritual, invisible nature. The earth on Banahaw is rocky and dense, rather inappropriate for planting and growing nourishment for the physical body. Mount Kristobal, on the other hand, is rich with fertile soil, attracting us to her land through the need to provide for our material existence. So we till her soil and plant on her, and in so doing, enter into a relationship with this dark side, fertile with possibilities to provide challenges to the ego. We wish neither to deny the existence of our dark side nor allow ourselves to be controlled by it.

"We all come to a place in our evolution where we must accept the challenge that Mount Kristobal offers us. It is the opportunity to face the reality that we are multifaceted beings, composed of both light and shadow. These two polarities are both capable of moving energy and influencing the quality of life, but the dark forces use control and manipulation to express themselves, while the light forces use surrender and vulnerability. If we do not face the dark side of our being and learn to master it, it will remain hidden in the subconscious where it is most potent and destructive. When we bring this part of our nature out of the subconscious and into the light, it is out of its element, and therefore less in control and unable to manipulate. The nature of light is such that it will eventually overwhelm the darkness, absorbing and integrating it into a perfect balance.

"So, perhaps you begin to understand the value and the necessity to bring out this darker side of our inner nature so that, through awareness, we can be free from manipulation and able to make our own choices. With this freedom, we have the opportunity to become whole, spiritually balanced human beings. Banahaw would be incomplete without its shadow just as our world could not exist without its polarities of heat and cold, joy and sorrow, day and night."

"Will we also climb Mount Kristobal?" I asked him.

"No. It is not necessary for a person to spend time on both mountains to receive these teachings because the mere viewing of these twins standing side by side reminds us of our own duality. When people enroll in the school of Mount Banahaw, if they have not yet come to terms with their demons and dark forces, they must face them as an initiation before they may go any further in their spiritual unfoldment. Mount Banahaw provides reflective pools, caves and waterfalls as tools to face our hidden depths, purge out the negativity and purify our souls so that we may become loving, balanced, intelligent human beings. The twin mountains are a physical demonstration of the absolute existence and the perfect harmony of the positive and negative poles of light and dark, the integration of life and death."

His words stimulated both my recognition and my fear. I began to wonder about myself, what inner battles I might have in store, and what parts of myself I had not yet come to terms with. The excitement of the past few days receded into the background while flashes of some of the darker enigmas of my dream worlds came to the forefront. I saw glimpses of the images that sometimes provoked me in the night, eluding my memory upon awakening. I shuddered at the thought that perhaps I would have the opportunity to meet these shadows head on.

The Jeep began to slow down and pulled up in front of a lovely wood-and-bamboo dwelling, with open sides inviting the air and sunlight to pour through. This area was quite different from the rest of the foothills. These homes were sturdily constructed with luxuries like bathrooms with plumbing. Several people strolled out from their domiciles to greet us. They seemed curious and pleased to discover me in their midst. I got the idea that foreigners were seldom brought here and I had a special feeling that I was being allowed into a secret world.

The maids began bustling around, unloading the Jeep and preparing the outdoor kitchen, when a painful cry sent Boy running over to the next house to investigate. Jimmy and I followed. We traced the sound to that of a screaming child who, we were told, had been thrown from a horse only moments before our arrival. His uncle was holding his arm, certain that it had been broken. Boy embraced the child and began to speak quietly to him, trying to calm him down a little.

I watched him systematically feeling carefully all the way up and down the child's arm. He stopped at a spot just beneath the elbow where the bone was angrily protruding from under the muscle. It was most definitely broken. While Boy gently soothed the child with his voice, he persistently manipulated the arm, until he was able to move the bone with his hands, placing it back into perfect alignment where it belonged. Where the protrusion had been only a moment before, it was now smooth. He had set the bone back in place and the child was beginning to relax a little. I was sure that he was still in pain, but since the arm no longer appeared grotesque, the child felt more secure. I thought about how wonderful it must feel to be able to help people like that. Perhaps through my upcoming apprenticeship with Tony, I would soon be able to alleviate pain like this.

Boy continued cradling the small child for some time until he had completely stopped crying and then put him and his uncle into the now empty Jeep, directing the driver to take them somewhere. They took off and he returned to us, smiling pleasantly.

"I have set the bone back in place but now he must go to the doctor to put the arm in a cast. The muscles are weak and the bone must mend. You see, when doctors and healers work together, then we can best serve the patient."

We returned to Boy's house and found the air thick with the unmistakable smell of Philippine cuisine: coconut oil heating up in great pots, the fishy odor of fresh seafood being cleaned and arranged for frying, and the tangy aroma of incomparable spicy native sauces stewing on the wood-burning stove.

Jimmy motioned for me to follow him and he led me on a short, silent tour of the immediate area. We listened to the melodious bird calls and outrageous insect sounds that seemed to come from invisible creatures hiding out in the trees and bushes. The earth was alive, the vegetation verdant and full, creating a profound feeling of balance and inner peace. I became aware that the nature forces were so strong that every living thing had surrendered to a natural rhythmic movement which I felt traveling through my own body. The more we strolled, the more harmonious I felt with my surroundings, and our walk became a moving meditation.

Jimmy stopped in front of a small shack and spoke for the first time since we had left Boy's house.

"I am taking you to meet Liwaway Pantas. Before she moved here, she was a city girl and worked as a schoolteacher. One day, ten years ago, someone brought her to this mountain for the weekend and she found that she had a very special connection with the place. She kept returning as often as possible, until one day she fell into a trance. Her spirit helpers came to her and instructed her to stop teaching school and to stay at the mountain full time. So she left her job, moved here, and devoted herself to spiritual development. It was difficult at first, because she had no money. When there was nothing to eat, she fasted, but often, a friend fed her or a member of her family sent her food and supplies. Somehow, the mountain always provided. She spent countless nights sleeping in the caves and communing with the spirits and teacher guides. She has become a powerful trance medium who can easily predict worldwide future events. She is also a guide who will lead us through our experiences here."

We knocked lightly and entered the hut, which was nearly empty of furnishings except for a wooden table and bench. Seated in the corner was a small, tiny-boned woman, who appeared to be about thirty or so. She smiled at us through dark, soft eyes, and I felt drawn in by the same invisible quality I had noticed on our way here, the energy that had seemed to pull us toward the place and make us a part of it.

Liwaway, or Waway (pronounced Wah-why), as Jimmy called her, appeared almost transparent, as if she weren't really taking up any physical space at all. Yet a decided air of self-confidence and composure defined her space quite clearly. With the delicacy of a deer she smiled at me. She made me feel safe. At the time, I did not realize how essential this quality was for a Mount Banahaw guide. I only knew that she projected warmth and that I felt comfortable in her presence.

She was obviously delighted to see Jimmy. When she stood to hug him, her thin, lanky body gave her the appearance of being taller than her five foot three inches. Jimmy filled her in on all the city news and when she listened, I had the sense that she was actually taking the words inside to feel them as well as hear them. When she spoke, her English was clear, precise, and easy to understand. She talked about the delicate balance required to thrive within this community and the political repercussions of trying to create an organized life-style among so many groups of people who did not necessarily share the same religious and social beliefs.

"The difficulties we experience here are due to spiritual ego. Each group that maintains a home here has a different basis for their practice," she said. "Most of them have a leader we call the 'Suprema' or 'Supremo' who sets the guidelines for that particular group. The majority of leaders are women, but whether they are male or female, when that leader feels that her or his way is better than any of the others, the egos clash."

We agreed that this was a common human behavior. Although we lived on different sides of the world, we shared a recognition of "one-wayism" to be a universal problem at the root of so much of the prejudice and dominance that has encouraged separation and war on our planet. We acknowledged that when people can accept themselves and each other as individuals and appreciate and learn from the differences, only then do we have a chance to live in peace. An hour passed quickly as we shared our views, which were amazingly aligned for belonging to such totally different societies. As we rose to leave, she assured us that she would meet us after lunch.

The appetizing smells of fresh fish, spicy chicken, fried pork, stewed vegetables, and mountains of white rice drew me eagerly to the house. My mouth watered and I realized that the invigorating mountain air had really whetted my appetite. I was ready to eat!

Lunch was a lively affair, filled with laughter, teasing, and great stories. We ate with gusto, using our hands more than the knives and forks that were provided. In a country where starvation is rampant, food is greatly appreciated, and a full belly means safety and abundance. When we were satiated, the maids cleared the table and ate the leftovers, peasant-style, squatting on their haunches just beside the cooking area. They gossiped and giggled in their native tongue and the undefined sound of it lulled me into a dreamy state. I dozed for a few minutes, briefly returning to the underground cave that I had dreamt of the night before. When I came to, Waway was sitting on the bench next to me.

Her presence startled me and I jumped, making everyone laugh.

"Andrea is already feeling the energy of the mountain," Boy teased, transforming his never-ending grin into a broad smile. "Perhaps it is time to explore."

Everyone agreed and although we left the house feeling

energetic and boisterous, we quieted down as we walked. We each went into our private thoughts, blending with the harmonious, rhythmic vibration that permeated us and everything around us. Waway's melodious voice floated through the air like a counterpart to the melody.

"We are on our way to Santa Lucia, the first of three initiations that one must experience before climbing the mountain. Negativity that has been stuffed down over many years can prove extremely dangerous, especially here. If this negativity is not cleansed out, the intensity of the high vibratory frequencies that exist in the caves and on the peaks of Mount Banahaw will purge too much too quickly. Without proper purification, the nervous system could literally burn up in the attempt to deal with all of these opposing energies. This afternoon will be one of cleansing and clearing the body and spirit."

Her words hit a nerve inside of me. I furtively looked at her and she returned my glance with a reassuring smile and a nod.

"I see that you are ready for the teachings here."

Once we passed through the clearings, the path narrowed and began a gradual uphill grade. As we started to climb and walking became more strained, I knew that my first lesson had begun. It was the issue of trust. I considered our strange-looking caravan: these small, dark, munchkin-like people, and me, light haired, blue-eyed, white skinned, towering above all of them. They were leading me to some unknown place that my friends back home had never even heard about. If I were lost or abandoned, no one would have the slightest idea where to start searching for me. I looked at Jimmy, who was quickly becoming a dear friend, at Boy, the Buddha-smile still hovering on the edges of his mouth and in his eyes, and gentle, doe-like Waway, with a face so open, she would be incapable of hiding even the tiniest lie. I was completely in their hands and I trusted them, partly because it was the only intelligent choice.

When we reached the top of the grade, the dirt path came to a halt. We began to descend into a deep canyon by way of precariously steep stairs of stone. The greenery bordering the steps was vivid and full, with errant branches brushing intimately against our legs. We walked silently and carefully, directing full concentration on the placement of our feet on the narrow, winding steps, still slippery from the residue of mud that had been deposited from incessant rains. As we got further away from the top, I had the feeling that I was being gradually swallowed by a giant mouth filled with earth, stone, and waving vegetation. Each step revealed more of the beauty of what was yet to come at the stomach of this seemingly endless abyss.

Suddenly the steps disappeared and we continued moving downward over the wet muddy earth. It took extreme muscular control in my thighs to remain in an upright position, for it was slippery and there was nothing to dig my feet into. I was feeling quite frustrated and tired when Boy pointed to a thick rope that had been tied from tree to tree along one side of the path, extending nearly all the way to the bottom of the canyon. I gratefully made my way over to the life-saving rope and grabbed on. While I walked heavily, using the rope for traction, I watched Waway step lightly down the slippery path in her rubber clogs as if she were wearing shoes that had been designed especially for mud-trekking. Her walk was carefree and focused, completely oblivious to any earthly hindrances.

The scenery was becoming more and more lush. I stopped quite often to rest my arms, which were feeling stressed from holding on to the rope, and looked around at my luxurious surroundings. I began to hear the muffled sound of rushing water and I knew that we were nearing the bottom of this vast canyon. My legs were shaking as the path took a final turn and stairs appeared once again, so narrow that I had to turn my feet sideways to make them fit. These were the final steps that spilled us out onto the canyon floor of this place called Santa Lucia. The magnificent reward for my taxing descent was now in clear view.

The panorama was so vast that I found myself turning in slow circles in order to take in the beauty that surrounded me.

The sides of the canyon shot up into the sky, bearing the weight of massive rocks and complex root systems of enormous, ancient trees. The entangled branches hung languidly down the walls of the canyon, being gently blown and caressed by the lazy, warm midday breezes. Looking up to see the culmination of these root systems strained my eyes. After living in the city for so long, my viewing range had been greatly limited and my eye muscles were unaccustomed to taking in so much at one time.

I kept looking up and up and up until I could see the tips of the trees, the place where the hilltops met the brilliant blue sky. The wavering shapes of the puffy, floating clouds kept expanding and transforming, reminding me of my favorite childhood game. My girlfriend and I would hold hands and lie down on the lawn, sniffing the aroma of the freshly cut grass. Staring at the sky and giggling constantly, we would find pictures in the cloud formations, trying to quickly describe them before they dissolved forever and turned into something else.

The sound of rushing water lured me back into the present and I watched waterfalls cascading down the sides of the canyon walls. Sparkling clear at the base of the falls, the pools were filled with people gathered for a common purpose: to heal their bodies and to receive the spiritual vibrations of energy present in the waters. Some were immersing themselves in a ritualistic fashion, praying and chanting, and others were just soaking and relaxing. Naked children played in the pools, but due to their strong religious morality, the men bathed in their shorts and the women wore both shorts and T-shirts or blouses. Splashes of color had been created by the placement of outer clothing on huge boulders which sat heavily and placidly in the pools. I was told later that during the rainy season, the storms are sometimes so fierce, they actually displace these enormous rocks, moving them to new positions. I followed closely behind Waway and Boy, as they approached one of the larger boulders, the entrance point to the sacred pools. Waway motioned for Jimmy and me to take a candle from her.

"This is the rock that houses the protective spirits of Santa

Lucia," she told us. "These spirits keep away low energies and transform the negative vibrations of the various ailments that are released as people bathe in the healing waters. Before we enter this space, it is customary to light a candle to honor the spirit presence, to acknowledge the sacredness of the work that is being done here, and to ask for protection and guidance."

I walked toward her on still-shaky legs and lit my candle. Closing my eyes, I was filled with deep gratitude for my guides, both physical and nonphysical, who I knew were taking care of me. I knelt in prayer and it occurred to me how much I had taken for granted in my life. When was the last time I had stopped for a moment to give thanks for just being somewhere wonderful or to honor the great work that was being accomplished? I recognized that the spirits were teaching me appreciation and I intended to embrace this as a valuable tool. Acknowledging the beauty of each moment can easily transform even the most mundane circumstance into something magical and stimulating.

When our prayers were complete, we stood and walked around the boulder. I followed my friends toward one of the sides of the canyon out of which an extremely complex root system was growing. A shimmering waterfall, sourcing high out of our field of vision, poured down through the roots and onto a level rock surface on the ground below. The water danced and sparkled, backlit by the sun, creating bouncing rainbow reflections for several feet around it. People were taking turns stepping up onto the natural rock platform, allowing themselves to be drenched by the cool, refreshing shower that was pouring down through the roots above.

Waway pointed out another waterfall, about ten feet away, also pouring through a thick entanglement of roots. "These are the roots of trees that grow at the very top of Mount Banahaw, the same place where these two waterfalls begin their descent. Many people think they can skip over physical purification and deal directly with Spirit, but it does not work so well. There is a perfect order in all things. We must first make our bodies strong so that we will have a powerful vehicle to handle the higher vibrations of Spirit. This is the gift that the waterfalls offer. When you stand under the water, allow it to completely wash your body and open your mouth to drink. This way, you will cleanse and purify the inside of the body as well as the outside. Besides, it tastes great!" And she flashed me a playful smile.

My legs still did not feel solid beneath me as I waded into the ankle-deep water. I walked with difficulty, trying not to trip over the sharp stones and pebbles that were almost invisible under the water. I rested my body on a sizable boulder and watched a man bathe his young child under the first waterfall. Her left eye was swollen shut and he was holding her head up so that the water would run directly into her face. It looked as if she were being splashed quite violently, but she was very calm and actually seemed to be enjoying herself. He was fervently praying for healing and I was touched by the deep love that he was expressing for his little girl.

When he finished his prayers, his path back to the pools led him very close to me and I reached out to touch the child's wet, shining black hair. She gazed at me directly and clearly, her good eye alive with light. For a few moments I could not move, I was so taken by her innocence and beauty. Suddenly she broke the stare as she threw her head back and laughed with such abandon that I forgot my shaky legs and my important cleansing mission and joined in her merriment.

I looked back to Waway who gave me a nod of encouragement. It was my turn to step under the waterfall. I waded carefully through the stones and stepped up onto the rock platform. A thrilling sensation of cold, rushing water drenched me from head to toe. I opened my mouth to gasp for air, and when I had caught my breath, I turned my head up to the shower and allowed it to run down my face and into my mouth. I swallowed the water and could feel it pouring down my throat and cooling my insides. Aware of being washed both inside and out simultaneously, I allowed every part of my body to be purified by this invigorating rite. The water traveling over different parts of my body produced alternating sensations of warmth and cold. The coldness made me feel tight and uncomfortable, as if the energy in that particular area were blocked. I breathed deeply into the iciness until my breath warmed me and my energy was flowing evenly and effortlessly. Then I simply stood and invited the water to flow completely over and through me, feeling like a clear, sparkling extension of the waterfall itself.

I had become completely lost in my shower when I remembered that I had friends with me awaiting their turns. I looked over at them and they were patiently standing by the rocks, quietly chatting with each other. I had the sense that they were deliberately leaving me to myself so that I could have my private moment in Santa Lucia. My heart swelled with gratitude and love for them and I stepped down from the platform, feeling clear and lively. As I made space for the next person to bathe under the water, I realized that my legs had acclimated to the environment. They felt solid and strong beneath me and the shakiness had totally disappeared.

I leaned back against the large boulder and felt that I was repeating my own shower as I watched Jimmy, Boy, and Waway bathe under the crystal clear waters. When they were finished, we waded over to the second waterfall and repeated the ritual. It was less shocking but equally refreshing and invigorating. My body balanced more quickly this time and I was able to breathe easily and deeply. When my second shower was through, I felt awake, alert, and ready for the long walk back to the world above.

I began impetuously bounding up the steps, but I controlled my overly excitable tendencies when I saw that my guides were once again walking slowly, falling into the natural rhythmic pace that the land encouraged. I followed their example and joined in the steady gait, conserving my energy and allowing myself to integrate with the earth and greenery around me. Because my legs were feeling strong and my body was balanced, it took no strain to keep myself moving, so the trip up was a great deal easier than the one down. In fact, it was so effortless and enjoyable that I was surprised at how quickly I found myself once again standing on the top of the stone steps of Santa Lucia.

As we began the walk to our next destination, a light, gentle rain sprinkled our bodies with a cool, refreshing mist. It felt like a continuation of the cleansing process that we had begun in the bottom of the canyon, but now it included the very Earth herself. Waway, coming up beside me, fell into perfect rhythm with my walk to inform me of our direction. I watched the tiny raindrops land on her face and bounce off into the sunlit space around her, filling her auric field with tiny, jumping rainbows. She spoke in her serene, reassuring way that had an almost hypnotic effect on me.

"I see that you are stronger now. Since we have cleansed our bodies, we are ready to move on to purification of the spirit. Our destination is Jacob's Well, the only mountain cave which contains a deep pool of water in its interior. This cave was inhabited for many years by a hermit named Mamay Pinoy, one of the first men to recognize the powers of Mount Banahaw. One morning, he disappeared under the water and everyone mourned him, believing that he had drowned. Imagine their surprise when he emerged three days later, saying that he had visited the ancient lost continent of Lemuria! From then on, he would disappear often, and upon his return he would delight the people of the mountain with amazing stories about this ancient and mysterious lost land. Many of our oldest legends are linked with his adventures, particularly in this very powerful Cave of Exorcism."

I felt a slight tinge of uneasiness at her words, but I let go as I listened to the sights and sounds around me. The birds called to each other in perfect unrehearsed harmony, making short, low flights from tree to tree, probably as interested in me as I was in them. Suddenly a high-intensity sound drew me to an abrupt standstill. It felt like an onrushing wave of static electricity that was answered by a resonant, melodious birdcall. Then there was silence for several seconds. Once again that undefinable sound rang out, followed by the same birdcall. Again, silence. These cries and answers continued to repeat themselves until I realized that I was inadvertently eavesdropping on an ongoing conversation between the insects and birds that inhabited the immediate area outside the cave of Jacob's well. The drizzling rain had stopped and we had arrived at our destination.

Intensity charged all of my senses at once, and I knew that we were no longer in the peaceful, nurturing atmosphere of Santa Lucia, that this was a completely different story. The rock formations made a difficult, jagged welcome mat. We climbed carefully across them until we reached the narrow opening to this dark, mysterious underground cave. A barefooted group of people stood there, quietly praying, waiting to go in next.

I looked at the opening to the cave and then at the thick body of a very heavyset woman preparing to enter. After some quick geometric calculations, I concluded that she was definitely larger than the area she was about to penetrate. It would certainly be impossible for her to fit through. Holding candles, they each disappeared into the blackness, the large woman taking up the rear. I was sure she would have to stop and wait for the rest to come back, but I was wrong. She took a deep breath, slithered between the rocks and was gone! My face must have been reflecting my astonishment, because I heard Boy lightly chuckling from behind me.

When I turned to face him, he grinned his immortal grin and said, "One has only to desire entry into Jacob's Well and it is done. It is said that the walls actually stretch to meet the required measurements, so no one who truly wishes this purification has ever been turned away. Fear gone out of control is the only emotion that can deter one's ability to pass through the opening."

While we quietly waited our turn, I felt the tension mounting inside of me. I didn't know exactly why, but each time I looked at the adjacent rocks that marked the entrance to this cave, adrenalin shot through me. I tried to divert my attention by focusing on the surrounding area, but my mind would inevitably return to the undisputed fact that soon I would be squeezing myself through that opening and entering a mysterious black hole that these people called the Cave of Exorcism.

Finally, the tip of the large woman's head peeked out from between the rocks. As the rest of her body squeezed out after her, I reassured myself that if she could get through this ordeal and emerge with all body parts intact, certainly I could, too. The rest of the group was close behind her, and finally were all standing outside the cave, looking wet and elated. They stepped to the side to dry off and make room for us. A powerful surge of fear pulsed through me as I realized that my turn had come.

My first impulse was to run to Waway and ask her a million questions. I wanted to know every single thing that was about to happen. What was inside that foreboding dark universe? Why did everyone emerge soaking wet? Why is it called the Cave of Exorcism? What were my chances of coming out alive? Couldn't I just skip this one? But I refrained because I knew that it was useless. I would get no satisfactory answers.

I understand now that "not knowing" is one of the basic ingredients of any true initiation. Successfully passing through an ordeal that is unknown to us builds one of the primary tools that serves us in most difficulties, the ability to trust. But the trust that I speak of is not about anything on the outside. It is trust of oneself. It is about the willingness to become vulnerable and place confidence in our own inner strength and guidance. This trust builds our innate, intuitive ability to know what is right for us and the courage to act accordingly, even if certain factors remain unknown.

Before I had any further chance to contemplate my next move, Boy approached the cave and took candles from a small bag he had been carrying. He turned to look at me. "I will go in first to light the way. When I call you, follow me. Okay?"

With his grin intact, he slid his small body in between the rocks and was gone from sight. I tried to look in after him, but the dark path seemed to swallow him as it curved down and around to the right, making it impossible to follow his progress. I shivered as an eerie glow of candlelight escaped the opening. In a few more seconds, I heard a slightly muffled voice, calling me to enter.

I looked behind me at Waway and Jimmy, who were preparing their own entry. Waway was praying as usual, and it didn't seem like a bad idea. I closed my eyes and prayed for the fortitude that I would need to complete this trial. I knew that my friends could feel my apprehension, for they gave me tender looks of encouragement. I placed my right foot in the small opening between the two entrance rocks. I had taken the first step!

I peered in and the first thing I saw was Boy's hand reaching up toward me. I gratefully grasped it and slid my body down through the narrow opening. Boy had set several candles along the walls of the cave so that I could see the indents for our feet. We were climbing straight down the sides of very steep walls and he showed me where to place each foot as I slowly followed him deeper and farther downward into this strange underworld. I was vaguely aware that Waway was close behind, but I never turned to look at her because I had to focus all of my attention on my footing. There were holes in the rock wall beneath me and the thought of slipping was terrifying because I had no idea what was at the bottom or if a bottom even existed.

Moving deeper within, my breath became shorter and my fear began to overtake me. The end was nowhere in sight, and we continued to make our way down, down, down, into the bowels of the earth. I wished that I could turn around and leave but it was too late. I knew that I mustn't panic because if I did, there was no way out. The only exit was the steep uphill climb the same way we had entered, and there were people behind me. I didn't even know if it was possible to climb back up.

Suddenly, the path took a sharp turn and I lost Boy's hand. As I turned to take my next step to follow him, I stopped abruptly. The walls were configured in such a way that there was almost no space for my body and no floor to stand on. My mind went into chaos as I saw that I would have to crouch and drop myself through this narrow crevice while I was balancing against the side of the wall. I froze in my tracks. My throat tightened so that I was choking off my own oxygen. I was out of control.

Then I heard it. When the sound of it filled the air, I came back to my senses. It was a song, so melodious, so gentle, re-assuring and nurturing that my mind stopped racing. I became aware that the choking feeling would leave if I would just breathe. Slowly, I began to take first a few short breaths and then several long, full ones. Everything in my body relaxed as I let go of my tightened muscles and allowed my weight to rest against the rocks behind me, breathing deeply and listening to the sound, a Spirit song that was coming from Waway's mouth. She sang in a tongue that I had never heard before and spoke words that I could not possibly understand, but I knew that I was all right and that I was safe and protected. I surrendered to the cave and released the rock that I was grasping for dear life. I allowed my body to drop down through that crevice, once again finding Boy's outstretched hand. In the next moment, I was safely standing on the rock below, catching my breath.

We continued to scale the sides of the walls until Boy directed me to stop. I watched him carefully as he lightly touched bottom and lit a final candle on the floor of the cave. I sighed relief as I learned that there actually was a bottom and that in a moment, I would be standing on it.

We had traveled about forty feet down and when I had both feet firmly planted on the earth beneath me, I directed my vision to the top of the cave where we had entered. I was dazzled by a bright beam of sunlight filtering down from the opening, lighting up the center of the floor of this underground world. Outlined in the brilliant light beam were two lizard people, whom I watched in amazement as they deftly scaled the walls of the cave as I had just done. When these reptilian-like creatures had reached their destination, they crawled off the walls and stood beside me. Waway and Jimmy had completed their journey and were transformed into human beings once again.

Waway turned to me and asked very simply, "Do you have claustrophobia?"

I could hardly believe her question. I felt infuriated and embarrassed and I wanted to scream out that maybe it was just a new experience for me to climb barefoot down cave walls in foreign countries with no idea what was at the other end, but I controlled myself and answered, "I guess so."

I tried to calm down, and, following Boy's example, I sat down on the dirt floor. There was ample space for everyone to sit comfortably and I attempted to control my breathing as challenging thoughts of my return climb assaulted me. I disciplined my mind to dismiss them, realizing that I had more immediate considerations, and I focused my attention on perusing my unfamiliar surroundings.

My eyes were slowly adjusting to the darkness of this underworld and between the light from the candles and the beam of sunlight from above, I could see quite clearly now. The circular-shaped floor of the cave was level and easy to walk upon, and at the side opposite the western entry point, the floor stopped abruptly, meeting a long, narrow body of water. The width of the water ran no more than three feet from where the floor stopped to the inside edge of the cave wall. This narrow expanse of water covered the entire east side, continuing its journey beneath us, extending further than anyone knew. It occurred to me that it might be possible to swim underneath the cave floor, but that thought was accompanied by a new bout of claustrophobia, so I erased it from my mind. A metal ladder extended downward into the well, reaching the water at the second rung.

Boy stood and approached the ladder.

"We will go down the ladder and completely immerse ourselves three times. This is how we purify our spirit. Pray that you may release all negative energies from your being and become renewed. I will go first so that I may greet you when it is your turn."

Turning to face us with his back to the wall, he started down the metal rungs. After he had taken about five steps, he let go and I watched his smile slowly disappear under the water. A few seconds later, he grabbed back onto the ladder and emerged, like the Cheshire cat, grinning from ear to ear. He appeared to be feeling wonderful, but how could I really tell? He seemed to like everything. He repeated the ritual twice more and, remaining in the stretch of water, immersed to his waist, he released the ladder and floated buoyantly over to the side and waited.

I wondered what he was waiting for when I noticed that everyone was staring at me. I shifted uneasily, knowing that it was my turn.

"How deep is it?" I called down to him.

His face lit up with joy.

"Nobody knows," he answered.

That was all I needed to hear. A surge of fear started at my feet and quickly traveled up my body until I was almost completely paralyzed. I looked from Waway to Jimmy, who were coolly looking back at me, patiently waiting for me to begin my descent into this bottomless pit of liquid blackness. To make matters worse, I saw Boy glance underneath the cave floor. My imagination went wild, creating pictures of having to swim under the cave to God knows where, with barely enough room to keep my head above water.

Somehow, I managed to get to my feet. By now I could barely breathe, but I thought that I could fake it and nobody would notice. I headed toward the ladder, turned my back to the wall of the cave and placed my foot on the first rung, just as Boy had done. When I reached the third rung, the chilling water swept across my knees, sending an enormous shiver through my nervous system. I lowered myself one more step, the water now playing with my waist. The higher the water rose to cover me, the more I felt my throat closing until I stopped on the last rung of the ladder, freezing, breathless, and panic-stricken. There was no way that I could move and I hung on for dear life, gasping for air as if someone or something were choking the life out of me.

It was my fear, amplified by my memory of the words that Boy had spoken at the cave entrance. "Fear gone out of control is the only emotion that can deter one's ability to pass through the opening." Well, I had made it through but as I hung there, immobilized by my fear, I doubted that I would ever be able to get out again. I was stuck in a terrible dilemma, terrified to step down any farther and physically unable to walk back up again. Everything inside of me felt frozen and out of control and I had no idea why I couldn't move. In that moment I was completely powerless, unable to do even the most basic thing in life, breathe. Feelings of humiliation and failure flashed through me. I felt completely alone and isolated in my prison of paralysis. I stayed there suspended in time and space and I prayed for help, for there was nothing that I could do to help myself.

Then I heard movement above me. I could not move my neck to look up but I managed to raise my eyes enough to see Waway walk to the edge of the cave floor. She looked down at me. When I locked into her stare, she opened her mouth and once again she sang. Her song floated gracefully through the air like the spirit of a fluttering, exotic bird and hovered by my right shoulder. Then it was inside of me, traveling through my body. My throat muscles relaxed first and then I was able to move my neck. I sobbed a quick breath as if it were the first I had ever taken. As the air filled my lungs, the paralysis slowly began to leave my body and movement returned to my frozen limbs. I breathed deeply; my fingers loosed their grip on the rung of the ladder. Waway continued her song and I looked over at Boy who was waiting beside me, smiling with encouragement. I was ready to carry on.

With a strong deep breath, I let go of the ladder and completely immersed myself in the freezing water. When I came up, I seemed to have emerged in a veil of fog, because when I opened my eyes, I was looking through a fine mist which had risen up all around me. It seemed to be coming from the water. Jimmy and Waway had come close to the edge and were looking down at me, fascinated by the instant weather change. The second time, I was able to stay under slightly longer. I emerged breathing easily and the air had cleared. My third dip was even more comfortable and when I was through, I climbed the ladder to the cave floor. My body collapsed to the ground. Cold water dripped off my skin and my clothing, mixing with the warmth of the cave air to create steam all around me. Relieved to have the attention off me, I regained my composure while Jimmy and Waway took their turns on the ladder.

When Waway had finished, she sat beside me and spoke quietly.

"If you want to spend the whole night in a cave, you must conquer your fear. Let's go down the ladder again. This time we can do it together," she offered.

Somehow, I had known that the ordeal was not yet over for me, so her suggestion did not surprise me. If I had survived once, then I could survive again.

"I'll go alone," I told her.

I approached the ladder and slowly turned to place my feet on the first rung. For a brief moment, fear swept over me like a gale of wind, but it was gone almost as quickly as it began. My fear transformed into sweet relief, and I stepped down the ladder. Lowering myself into the well, I immersed my body three times, my free-flowing tears merging forever with the water.

The ascent back to the world of light was effortless and relaxed. I felt that I was carrying out a completely different body than the one with which I had entered. Although I was trembling from the cold, it was only affecting me on the outer surfaces, because a sense of warmth and well-being flooded my insides. I was speechless, filled with gratitude that I had survived the ordeal. Waway's song had been a lifeline from her spirit to mine and I felt that she had saved my life.

"You have experienced an initiation into power," Boy told me as we dried ourselves off outside the entrance of the cave. "Perhaps now you have an idea of what I meant when I spoke of the challenge of power. Waway's song was a gift that you could have refused but you opened yourself to trust her. That was a good choice because through that opening, you received the strength and energy that you needed to proceed. If you had chosen to refuse her offering, it would have been impossible to gain the confidence that you found in the well. It was only through surrender and trust that you were able to face the hidden parts of your being that were stopping you from experiencing your true personal power.

"With each new level of consciousness that we reach, the ego is challenged to see if we have the courage to surrender enough to handle the higher intensities of vitality and truth that that level brings to us. If we choose to resist, we will be stuck for as long as it takes us to face our fears. When we finally surrender, we are purified, for we have given ourselves the opportunity to know the truth and to release our illusions. This release provides us with the capacity to accept ourselves as we are and to accept the degree of power we hold. When power is embraced as a concept of surrender, all that it asks in return is that the individual be dedicated to prayer and inner centering. Truly powerful people are balanced, trusting, and compassionate, with a highly developed understanding of who they are."

I walked on in silence, no longer needing to know what was coming next and feeling no fear. I had finally surrendered myself and I gracefully proceeded in a state of trust.

12

DREAM CAVE

I'm slowly walking along a short corridor, touching the low dirt ceiling and walls as I go. They are wet and soft and I like the sensuous feeling of the malleable earth between my fingers and under my nails. I recognize that I am in a small cave but, although it seems familiar to me, I know that I have never been here before. All of my senses are alert and I am waiting for something. I don't know what it is, yet I feel safe and unhurried. I am certain that I am exactly where I should be.

I sit quietly and look at the rich brown earth around me. The light tapping of droplets of water falling from the roof and rhythmically hitting the cave floor have a hypnotic effect on me. My mind is clear and relaxed as I sit in meditation. Although I am waiting, I am in a profound state of peace. Watching a transparent wave of light floating toward me, I am completely still and unafraid. As it begins to take form, I try to make out who or what it is but the light is blinding me. My eyes become heavy and it is too much effort to keep them open.

I awakened facing the west with the setting sun glaring into my eyes. For a moment I fought to keep them open, shielding the light with my arm, trying to remember what I was looking for. I knew that it was something extremely important, but, not being able to recall what it was, I gave up and turned my back on the intense glare. Feeling heavy and displaced, I sat up on the sleeping mat, blinking my aching eyes. Looking around, I gradually remembered where I was.

I was resting in the house at the foot of Mount Banahaw and I sighed relief when I saw Boy and Jimmy napping on their mats near me. I wiped the perspiration off my neck and forehead and laid back down to gather my thoughts. I nuzzled my head affectionately into the pillow, appreciating the fact that I was warm and alive. The far-off sound of the giggling maids and the familiar aroma of dinner preparations provided a reassuring background.

This was the third time I had dreamed of that cave. I wondered where it was and what significance the dream held for me. It was definitely not one of the caves we had already visited.

Our last stop had been the Cave of Presentation, which is actually two caves sharing a middle wall, with a common, easily accessible entrance. Waway had informed me that this duplex-like formation was the home of the spirits of Saint Peter and Saint Paul. We had climbed down a short ladder and entered the first side, in which stood a beautiful altar with many candles burning. I was to light a candle, place it on the altar, and present my name to the spirits, who would then record me in their invisible golden book. I would then be officially accepted as a student in the school of Mount Banahaw. Waway told me that when a person's psychic powers are developed, they can physically see the spirit book and their name entered within.

After sitting on the rocks at the back of the cave for a few moments, which were naturally formed like pews in a church, I had approached the altar. Feeling extremely emotional, I gratefully offered my candle and asked for acceptance into this magical and powerful school. When I felt that I had received acknowledgment, I walked the short distance into the other half of the cave to repeat the process. The ritual had been warm and satisfying, and I had come away with a strong sense of acceptance and completion.

Sleeping mats had already been placed on the floor when we returned to the house, and I remembered quickly sinking onto one of them and instantly falling into the peacefulness of my dream world.

The sun was getting lower in the sky as I pulled myself up from my sleep, shaking out the kinks in my legs. I walked outside the hut and stood transfixed, watching a magnificent sunset color the entire sky, transforming the cloud formations on the tip of Mount Banahaw into shining rainbows.

I watched the ever-changing sunset dance with the sky, and I saw that my experiences in the caves paralleled this palette of color that was playing with the world around me, causing everything to look different from moment to moment. When I turned my face to meet the sunset, I could actually feel the colors and vibrations from the earth coming up through my feet, traveling up my spine, and flowing throughout my entire body, feeding me tremendous vitality.

I tuned in to the centers in my body, called *chakras,* where the energy concentrates in powerful vortices. I could feel this energy spinning out from within me, moving blockages and opening me to higher frequencies of light and understanding. Similar to those centers in the body, there are many such areas on our planet emanating extremely high vibrational frequencies, which produce challenging and transforming experiences. People travel long distances to reach these geographical power spots in order to heal physical blockages, balance the emotions, and increase psychic abilities. The tingling vibrations traveling through me let me know that I was standing on one of these energy vortices.

Pictures of the events that had occurred since my arrival at the mountain flooded my mind and I began to see the logical way in which nature had created this power spot. Each area which held a particular psychic teaching actually took on the physical form of that lesson.

The first view of Mount Banahaw is with her shadow, Mount Kristobal. The sight of them standing side by side represents the first teaching, the harmonic marriage of the dark and light sides of our being.

The deep canyon of Santa Lucia cannot be reached without an arduous climb downward in which the physical body is heavily exercised and challenged. This forecasts the process to come of energetic movement and physical clearing. Once inside the canyon, we stand under waterfalls that begin at the highest and clearest point of the mountain, and so carry with them the highest and clearest healing vibrations. The waterfalls empty into pools which run off in a top current, flowing downstream away from the mountain, representing the release of our surface ailments that may have been blocking our physical health. Once cleansed, we are inspired to climb back up the canyon with lightness and speed, very different from the heaviness we felt as we descended. In this way, nature has skillfully arranged a demonstration of our newfound vitality, so that our brains can swiftly imprint the information that we have indeed experienced healing of the physical body, the gift that Santa Lucia offers.

The deeper inner teaching of the next initiation is physically forecasted by the change from the sunlight and openness of Santa Lucia to the shadowed pathways and densely growing vegetation along the way to Jacob's Well. At the cave's entrance, the bumpy rock formations are already forcing us to tread lightly and carefully, letting us know that we must proceed with caution. The opening to the inside is narrow and dark, and we squeeze ourselves into the unknown as if we were finding our way to the very depths of our own mysteries, which in truth we are. The pathway to the well is filled with challenges and shocking surprises, just as the way to our subconscious mind is filled with hidden obstacles that must be overcome. Once we have penetrated the subconscious and found ourselves at the depths, we are faced with a seemingly bottomless emotional body, physically represented by the bottomless well of water at the floor of the cave.

If we have not faced our essential truths, immersion into the cold water will purge our fear, triggering whatever hidden emotions have been stored away and forgotten. If we can only remember to look up, the rock formations at the entrance of the cave have provided an opening for a radiant beam of sunlight to stream in from above, reminding us that the higher sources of light are ever-present, even when we are facing our darkest trials. The emotions are confronted, expressed, and released in the depths of the well, and there, as the water flows out in an undercurrent, the negativity is carried away. In this way, the subconscious blockages are released and purged. The final journey out of the blackness of this underworld and up toward the light is an expression of our commitment to change the direction of our lives from that of dying to one of living.

The initiations are three, forming a triad which represents the integration of body, spirit, and mind. The third and last leg is the Cave of Presentation, where we outwardly communicate the inner awarenesses that the mind has integrated. This dual cave is easily accessible and represents the dual nature of our life on earth. We simply walk down a few steps and we are in either section. This is the place where we speak our names to the saints, allowing us to be identified and to offer our personal appreciation to the powers that inhabit this sacred mountain. This cave is chapel-like, with natural boulders serving as seats that face the beautifully ornate rock altars at the front. As our sole purpose is one of offering our vulnerability and prayers to the spirits, both sides of the cave are oval-shaped, with all of the energy moving toward the altar as it does in churches and cathedrals.

As a result of what I had gone through, the material plane began to appear to me as a mirror reflection of the subtler, higher frequencies which are constantly influencing and shaping the consciousness. My initiation had afforded me a deeper connection with nature, so that I could see how naturally the physical and nonphysical dimensions are integrated. By getting more in touch with myself, my psychic awareness was automatically opening and giving me a more ecstatic and linked experience of life on this earth. I silently spoke my gratefulness and remained in the glow of the sunset, allowing the colors to wash me with their radiance.

The sun had almost disappeared from view when the buzz of giant mosquitoes, licking their lips at the smell of white flesh, reminded me that it was time to change into long pants. I went inside and found the maids once again bustling around and piling the table with tasty Philippine delicacies. They invited me to eat and as I took my seat, Waway appeared at the door of the hut. I was overjoyed to see her, and she came in and sat down next to me to join us for dinner.

We had been eating for only a few minutes when I heard someone calling Boy's name. A tall man with sparkling eyes appeared at the open entrance of the house, laughingly saying something in Tagalog. Boy greeted him with great joy and invited him to enter. He limped in and threw his long body on the seat facing the table. He was holding his calf muscle, grimacing and laughing at the same time. Boy got up from the table and sat beside him, taking the leg in his hand and tuning in to the muscle.

Boy explained, "This is my good friend. He and his family have the house next door and his name is also Boy. We call him Boy M. He has what you call a charley horse in his calf. Maybe he has been thinking too much." They both burst out laughing, and Boy M.'s eyes lit up so brightly I thought they would blind me. Their laughter was extremely contagious, and we all joined in the merriment.

Boy M. looked at me, leaned forward, and with a devilish grin said, "You see, many people come here to suffer for their sins, but we don't really believe in sins. We come here to celebrate." They obviously thought that this was the funniest thing that they had ever heard, because they began to hoot with laughter again. I watched Boy Fajardo massaging Boy M.'s leg and I could see how much they were enjoying each other's company and how close they were. They looked totally different physically, Boy M. being close to six feet tall with a deep voice and wild, dark eyes. He looked like a fighter. Boy F. seemed more settled, more at peace with himself and ready to take what came. And yet, they shared their attitudes of joy. To these two men named Boy, life really was a celebration. I was delighted to be with them.

I ate heartily and although my friends were chatting away in their native tongue and I could not understand the words, I felt that I got the gist of everything that was transpiring. I was enjoying a new lightness of spirit, and I listened to them rattling on in a mixture of Tagalog and English, an off-beat dialect that the Filipinos themselves have humorously named "Taglish." Boy F. finished massaging his friend's leg and rejoined us at the table. Boy M. stood and walked easily to the door, the charley horse completely gone.

He turned to face me as he was leaving and said, "It seems that man has deteriorated from having the ability to heal himself. He has digressed to needing touch from another, and finally to using medicines, metal tools, and electronic machines. Self-healers flow with nature, so it is good that you are at Mount Banahaw to become more in touch with nature and yourself." He left to join his family.

When I was too full to eat any more, I sat back to take a breather. Waway, who had been picking daintily at her food, as if she were a bird, turned to me and said matter-of-factly, "You are a Lemurian. That is why you are here."

Recognition coursed through my body at her words. I had been intrigued when I heard that the healers felt that the ancient lost continent of Lemuria was their heritage. There were very few books written about it and even the ones that I had seen contained limited information. But something about Lemuria struck a chord within me. I had felt like an alien for most of my life, not totally out of touch with my surroundings but never quite belonging either. Tonight, 9,000 miles from my homeland, sitting with these people who were outwardly so different from me, I was being called a Lemurian and I felt truly at home for the first time in my life.

Jimmy took my hand and explained to me, "We who come to Mount Banahaw believe that when the continent of Lemuria sank into the ocean, the uppermost tip remained above water. This is the Philippines as you know it today. Within this Holy Mountain there are several entrances into the still thriving underground civilization of Lemuria. Jacob's Well is one of them. The Lemurians were a race of people who had highly developed psychic abilities beyond those of any other race known to man. The psychic healers, along with those who inhabit this mountain, believe themselves to be direct descendants from this race and they retain the ancient abilities. You have come home."

I started to cry and I closed my eyes to give a silent prayer of thanks for being delivered back home again. Images of the cave that had been haunting me appeared once again in my mind. I described these dreams and visions to my friends in detail, including the rhythm of the dripping water, the way the walls looked, and how I had felt sitting inside and meditating.

Waway sat back, closed her eyes for a few minutes and then announced, "I know where we will sleep tonight. You have dreamed of the Crown of Stone. This cave is calling to your spirit."

I asked no questions, for after my experience in Jacob's Well, I had built a strong trust for Waway. The sun had fully set, allowing the moon to peek out and begin to cast its luminescent glow, lending even more of a sense of enchantment to this magical land. Boy, Jimmy, and Waway made preparations for our night in the cave. I felt a bit dubious about climbing the mountain in the dark but since it didn't seem to be a concern to anyone else, I controlled my doubts, busying myself with changing my clothes and getting ready for the hike. We took flashlights, blankets, and sweaters because the night air was becoming cool. Jimmy looked at me to see if I was ready. As our eyes met, I could see, to my surprise, that he looked ill at ease, slightly nervous and unsure. He whispered to me, "Although I have been here many times, this will be my first time to sleep in a cave in Mount Banahaw."

We climbed slowly and steadily up, falling into the rhythmic walk with which I had become familiar. The ground was dark and full of sharp rocks and holes. The three of them carried our only flashlights, and I found myself once again in a vulnerable position. I felt dependent upon my friends, literally not being able to move until they lit up the earth for me. These basic themes of trust and surrender were recurring and I had to pay attention and try to let go of my desire to be in control.

There were many deep holes in the earth through which one could fall and be seriously injured. The moon had risen high in the sky by now, lending a dream-like quality to our surroundings. Our bodies cast long, distorted shadows on the ground, looking more like reflections of space creatures than human beings. Our caravan stopped at various designated locations, usually in front of rock altars and caves, and Waway would kneel and pray to the resident spirits, asking for blessings and protection.

In the diffused light of the moon, I caught sight of an arched entrance of a vaguely defined dark structure. With the moonlight reflecting off the top, the stones which bordered the opening looked exactly like a glittering jeweled crown. I knew this had to be the Crown of Stone and I was anxious to see how the reality of the place compared with what I had seen in my dreams.

But I waited while Waway once again did her prayer and chanting ritual, assuring our welcome by the Goddess of the Sea, the
protective spirit of this particular cave.

Waway smiled at me with her moonlit eyes and motioned
that I might now enter the cave. Boy remained standing behind
her, his white teeth glowing in the dark. Finally, I looked at
Jimmy to see if he would come with me, but he stepped back,
allowing me first entrance. This time I was not afraid. The
passage under the top of the crown was tall enough to allow
me to step through with several feet to spare above my head.

Entering slowly, I could see by the moonlight glow that the
cave floor was full of large jutting rocks, so I walked with care,
gently brushing my hands along the walls, reveling in the sensuous, soft, wet texture that I had felt in my dreams. I moved
as if I were floating several feet above the ground, and I lost
the sense of whether I was awake or asleep. At one point, I
heard the rhythmic sound of dripping water and I looked to
my left, seeing the familiar droplets falling from the roof and
steadily hitting the cave floor.

It was only about ten feet from front to back and I had no
idea how long I walked back and forth, stroking the walls, in
my trance-like state. When I finally emerged, Waway and Boy
were laying out blankets. The ground in front of the cave had
the same kind of large protruding rocks that were inside, and
I wondered where we would sleep. I was careful to keep my
considerations to myself but Jimmy loudly voiced our shared
apprehension.

"How in the world are we supposed to sleep on these rocks?
It will be impossible!" he complained.

Waway looked at him with her penetrating gaze.

"We do not come to the caves to sleep. We can do that in
bed. We come here to commune with the nature spirits."

Not another word was said as we sat on the blankets and
quietly went into reverie, looking at the moon and breathing in
the cool, clean night air. Little by little, I found myself moving
into a state of peace. All questions and considerations fell away

and I tuned into a sense of perfection, an absolute knowledge that I was precisely where I was meant to be.

We began to speak quietly, sharing our views of life and personal freedom. Each word that came out of anyone's mouth felt like my own, the feelings expressed were also my feelings, until I no longer knew or cared if it was I or someone else who was speaking. We talked well into the night in perfect harmony and communion. The liquid light of the moon and the balmy feeling of the air made me feel as if my body had been transported to another world, that I might have landed in someone else's dream.

When I began to feel slightly drowsy, Jimmy announced that he wanted to rest. Waway suggested that since the cave was too small to fit all four of us, she and Boy would remain out in front under the stars. Jimmy and I could sleep inside. In a few hours we would trade places. We picked up our blankets and carried them into the cave.

The jutting rocks were even larger within the cave than outside it, and we sat upon this hard, uncomfortable surface, with only a thin blanket between us and the cold, piercing rocks below. We stared with disbelief at each other, amazed at the concept that anyone could possibly be deluded enough to think that we could sleep in here. There was just enough space for the two of us to lie down with our bodies pressed against each other and the sides of the cave. We shifted around for a few minutes, doing our best to arrange ourselves so that sharp edges were not sticking into our vital organs, but to no avail. The ground was a nightmarish bumpy surface with no way to adjust ourselves to comfort. I closed my eyes, feeling terribly upset and disappointed, enduring the pain of the rocks which were cutting into my kidneys each time I breathed. This was not at all how I had imagined my night in the caves. It suddenly occurred to me that I no longer heard the dripping water, and I realized to my dismay that the sound had been silenced by my own body, graciously catching each drop as it landed.

I turned to face Jimmy, feeling my entire right side being

slowly and steadily soaked with cold water. At the same moment, he turned to me and we spontaneously broke out into intense laughter. Here were the two city folk, completely out of our element, braving the nature forces, kidneys aching, soaked by dripping water, and trying to appear nonchalant. We laughed hysterically at ourselves, at each other, and at "another fine mess" we had gotten ourselves into. The laughter was the perfect medicine, for it released tension and took our minds off of our discomfort. When we calmed down, I noticed that I had allowed my muscles to relax, the body pain had lessened, and the rocks were a little bit easier to deal with.

We lay there for a long time, smiling at each other, and the longer I looked into Jimmy's eyes, the more linked with him I became, until I felt as if I were spontaneously floating out of my body, looking at him from another dimension. His body became transparent and, looking straight through him, I suddenly had the strange sensation that I was seeing life through his eyes and feeling each emotion that he experienced. It took me a few moments to get my bearings and then I knew that I had moved inside of him and I was actually linked with his soul.

I hovered in this strange reality, taking in the world from this new perspective. I knew who he was and who he had been, his greatest joys, sorrows, and desires, his wisdom and his imbalances, and I was compelled to speak about what I could feel and perceive from within him. He caught his breath, speechless, and listened to my expression of his soul. He was being cracked open and probed and he cried from both embarrassment and relief that his deepest secrets were being exposed to himself and another human being.

When his hand reached out to grab mine, I felt as if I were making contact with myself. His experience of caressing my skin became my own. As our souls had joined, it was only natural that our bodies do the same. The energy was so great when we merged together that there was no separation between us. And we were not only together with each other; we were in communion with all of the nature forces and the floating spirits that surrounded us.

I lightly floated back into my own body, slightly disoriented as if I had been asleep and was now awakening in a familiar place. I could not tell who was more surprised and overwhelmed. Jimmy and I once again looked into each other's faces, tears falling down our cheeks, knowing that we were forever linked in soul and spirit.

Once back home within myself, I was aware of the rocks still rudely pressing into me, but the impact of the pressure had greatly diminished. The ground became less intrusive until it miraculously softened and molded to the shape of my body. When I finally stopped resisting them, the rocks and I merged together, and I gently drifted off into an enchanted sleep.

I am lying on the floor of the Crown of Stone. My eyes are closed, yet I can see everything around me. The sides and ceiling of the cave are there, but they seem rather vaporous. Although I do not turn to look at him, I know that Jimmy is lying next to me. I am very attracted to a white, misty form beginning to take shape above my head. I recognize it as the form that had appeared in my previous dream, but this time, the light does not blind me. I see it slowly solidifying into a woman who is floating in midair. She is radiantly beautiful, wearing long, flowing white skirts, and her arms are outstretched directly over both Jimmy's head and mine, as if she were blessing us. A projection of energy emits from her hands that is so soft and loving, I feel I am being stroked by feathers or clouds. I know that she is not sad, but water is literally pouring from her eyes and as I look into them, I feel as if I am being drawn into the sea. I exchange a deep communion with this spirit and gratefully receive her blessings.

A sudden bright flash of white light hit my face and I awakened with a start. I sat up quickly and looked around to see what was happening. The entire sky was bright as day and I saw Waway also sitting up from her resting place in front of the cave, staring into the heavens. As quickly as the light had appeared, it was gone, leaving the world in darkness. Then, several seconds later, the phenomenon recurred, bringing unannounced daylight into the sacredness of the black night. It lasted long enough for me to see that both Jimmy and Boy were still sleeping peacefully, completely undisturbed. The second disappearance of the light returned the night to its former darkness. I waited to see if the flash would repeat, but the show was over and all was as before.

I draped my blanket around me and quietly rose, shivering both from the memory of the dream and the dampness of the cave. I walked out to sit beside Waway, hoping she might be able to explain this strange light phenomenon that we had just witnessed.

She seemed unconcerned. Still looking up at the sky, Waway asked me, "Do you believe in dreams?"

"Of course," I replied.

"The caves inspire the dream in us. I have had a dream and now I know why I am here with you. I have seen the protectress of this cave, the Goddess of the Sea. She materialized inside the cave in long, flowing skirts, floating over your heads, blessing you. She was crying because she is very happy. She told me that, long ago, when you were here before, you and Jimmy made an agreement to return to this place to reconnect your souls with hers once again. I was chosen as the guide that would bring you here. I am also very happy because I have helped you to fulfill your destiny."

I stared into the night, wondering if I was really hearing these words or if I was still asleep, inside the cave. If her perception of the dream was true, perhaps it explained why I had dreamt of the cave before I ever saw it: I had already visited here in another time.

"I have had the same dream," I replied. "Do you think that

dreams of future events could be nothing more than memories of the past?"

Waway nodded her head, not at all amazed or surprised at my question. I supposed this was not the first time that she had participated in inexplicable events at this enchanted mountain. It seemed that she had reached a stage at which she questioned nothing, merely accepting it all as it came.

Both Jimmy and Boy had begun to stir as we spoke, and we all congregated in front of the cave. I spoke of the strange light flash that I had seen. Jimmy informed me that it was undoubtedly UFO activity. Many sightings and encounters had been reported from the peaks of this mountain over the years. No one even questioned them anymore.

"We will change places now," Waway said. "I want to offer my prayers to the Goddess." She and Boy entered the cave and Jimmy and I lay down in the open air where the rocks were flatter and spaced farther apart. It was a great deal more comfortable and I quickly dropped off to sleep.

> *I am standing in the center of a group of Banahaw women. They are friendly but slightly removed, not sure about my presence. One of them steps forward and asks me, "Why are you here?"*
>
> *I know that she is not looking for the answer to the question. She wants to know if I am aware of the true reason for my being amongst them.*
>
> *I speak unhesitatingly. "My spirit was called here and I have answered."*
>
> *"Yes." She and the rest of the women exchange nods of agreement. "It is as we have been told." And they softly walk away.*

When I opened my eyes, the sun was high in the sky. My friends were awake, picking up the blankets and clearing the area from the night before. I stood up, stretching and yawning, admiring the magnificent view that I had not been able to see in the darkness of the night. I picked up my blanket, feeling a growing hunger gnawing at my insides.

"I'm starving! I hope it doesn't take too long to get back to the house," Jimmy announced. I laughed, amazed at our connection and his habit of speaking out what I was thinking. We began our descent, making our way down the mountain with ease and assuredness, passing various groups of people who had spent the night in the caves. As we were nearing the bottom, a woman stepped out of the shadows and faced me. I recognized her as the same woman who had questioned me in my dream. But this time she was smiling.

"How did you like your night on Holy Mount Banahaw?" she asked.

"I liked it very much," I replied. We stood for several moments, smiling into each other's eyes. She nodded her approval and walked back into the shadows.

We continued our descent, and as we hit level ground, I breathed in the freshness of the morning air and took Jimmy's hand. We walked silently together, following our noses to the house where the rich aroma of hot coffee and a hearty breakfast were awaiting our return.

Mount Banahaw is one of the uncommonly rare places in which the invisible spirit world lives in harmony with the denser physical world. It is truly enchanted, and not necessarily available to everyone, due to its unique relationship with space and time. It is we, the earth dwellers, who actually keep such places within our reach. Our thought forms and our desires to share the knowledge of the unseen dimensions give us access to them.

If people were to abandon the area and deny support to the invisible realms, these realms would lose their bonding to the earth and slowly withdraw into inaccessible vibrational frequencies. Their teachings and beauty would be lost to us forever. The pilgrims of Mount Banahaw feed the spirit realms by offering prayer and respect, the sustenance that is needed to bridge the gap between the worlds. Our dreams are a way in, showing us not only places that might be impossible to reach with our physical bodies, but also symbols and images that the rational mind could not otherwise fathom. Dreams are a mirror reflection of our connection to the invisible worlds, a miraculous opportunity to meet the truth if we can be courageous enough to face ourselves.

As Waway so aptly stated, the caves inspire the dream in us. When we enter a cave, we move from the light into the darkness. Similarly, when we dream, we leave the waking states to move into the depths of the subconscious. The caves are actually a physical expression of our subconscious mind, the circular womb-like darkness acting as a stimulant to our own inner world of creation.

It was a dream that led me to my own depths in Mount Banahaw and since then, I see life itself as a dream, with each state of consciousness a further awakening into higher awareness. The essence of Mount Banahaw will always remain one of my most powerful living dreams, providing strength for my body, stimulation for my mind and nourishment for my spirit.

13

OBSESSION

The awakening of my subconscious was dramatic. Upon my return to Manila, I described all my adventures in full detail to Lois, then neatly placed them in my treasure chest of dreams. They lay there waiting for me to sleep, when they would burst open in full Technicolor and relive themselves. Areas which I had previously feared and avoided became my greatest draw. I lost contact with my physical body and my appetite waned. I felt languid in my waking states and I could hardly wait to sleep so that I could visit these secret dream treasures that I had locked away in the other world. Lois expressed concern about my well-being but I assured her that I had never felt better.

In the meantime, we began our immersion into the healing work, and our involvement with Tony took precedence over everything else. We spent the next couple of weeks traveling between Alex's and Tony's house, hungrily devouring any information that came our way. Following Tony's direction, I watched Alex's hands very carefully while I was assisting, and made some interesting observations. He only penetrated the flesh about forty percent of the time. The rest of the time, he magnetically brought up the blood or tissue, allowing it to materialize on the skin and then removing it. I told Tony what I had seen and he confirmed that my observations were correct. It was not always necessary to operate. He told us that toward the end of our stay, he would give us a chance to practice.

I spent sleepless nights in anticipation, alternating between fear and excitement, always wired and impatient for the next day to arrive. When I did manage to sleep, I was transported to Mount Banahaw. I would crawl into the caves and visit with the new parts of me that had surfaced, always seeing the faces of Jimmy, Boy, and Waway watching me from nearby. I knew that I was a little bit out of control, but I couldn't seem to do anything about it and I didn't really want to. I had decided that doing psychic surgery was the most important thing in the world and if I did not accomplish my goal, my life wouldn't be worth much. Somewhere inside I knew how ridiculous that was, that I was just obsessed and that my attitude was unhealthy. But my ego paid no attention, pushing me onward and telling me that when I accomplished my goal, I would be completely fulfilled and happy. I had convinced myself that if I could just do this one thing, the rest of my life would be perfect. Nothing else seemed to matter anymore. Even sleep did not remove me from the constant grinding of my mind. But I did not try to stop it. I took the liberty of totally absorbing myself in my obsession.

Lois, on the other hand, stayed true to form, enjoying her work and relaxing in her spare time. She slept well, ate well, and although she could see the craziness I was putting myself through, she left me alone. I guess she knew that if she interfered, it would do me no good. She let me be myself and through it all, we remained very close. The only reference she made to my obsessive behavior was, "You are strong and gifted, with your whole life ahead of you. Don't forget who you are."

The harder I worked, the more anxious I became. A strange feeling of emptiness and futility overcame me. What if there wasn't enough time to accomplish my goal? I couldn't bear the thought of returning home like an ordinary person, unable to achieve what I had set out to do. I hated being ordinary. I wanted to be special, to do something that no one else could do. Deep down inside, I had always felt that I was chosen for something more than the mundane life of an average person. There must be a reason that I was here, learning from these extraordinary people. I was sure that I was meant to be like them. Then, my life would have the meaning that I felt it was meant to have. I was fiercely determined. I simply had to do it.

Three days before we were to leave the Philippines, we went to Tony's for the last time. He had promised that this was the day he would let us practice psychic surgery. Lois was excited and I had hardly slept the night before, because I felt that this was my last chance to prove myself. I thought that if I failed, I would be going home with nothing more than I had when I arrived here. I walked determinedly up Tony's old, creaky wooden stairs, said a prayer, and entered the living room.

The smell of garlic and fish met us at the door. The Romero family was in the kitchen having breakfast. Tony greeted us, gave us a hug and asked, "Did you take your *breakfast?*"

I shook my head, suddenly becoming aware that, although Lois had gone down to breakfast, I had eaten nothing that morning. He ushered us into the kitchen and we sat down with his family. Teresa and their youngest son got up to make a place for us. I was not hungry and I hated disturbing their meal, but I knew that there was no use in protesting. Their greatest joy was to serve others. They heaped a plate with garlic rice and fried fish and placed it in front of me. Tony leaned toward me, his mouth full of rice, and whispered, "This healing work that you are doing takes much energy. Let me give you a hot *tif.* Here's the *scoof.* Keep your stomach *pull!*" He went back to his food and, even in my overwrought state, I choked from holding in my laughter at his bizarre way with words.

The other two children soon excused themselves from the table. They were off to school and Lois and I topped off our feast with a couple of bananas and went into the living room to prepare for the patients. Tony sat behind his table, lit up a cigarette, and looked at me through his deep eyes which always seemed to pierce right through me.

"I have consulted the Holy Spirit and He told me I can give you everything. Today I will allow you to practice on someone's stomach because the flesh is soft and easy to enter. When a patient arrives who needs a stomach *oferation,* you, Seester Andrea, will be the first one to do it."

I could feel my body shaking in anticipation. I tried to calm down while I sat and waited, every nerve in my body alert to the sounds, listening for the arrival of the stomach that would change my life. I closed my eyes and felt a mixture of impatience and dread, both anxious and fearful that someone might actually arrive. There were no patients for about a half hour. The wait was unbearable.

Finally, the inevitable occurred. I heard the bell ringing downstairs and the dogs began their relentless din of welcome. An older man, leaning on a young boy, limped into the room and sat on the bench. Although it was still early morning, the day was already boiling hot and the two guests were dripping with perspiration. Tony switched on a fan, which began to monotonously turn from one side to the other, teasing us with a quick, cool gust and then accentuating the stifling heat as it blew in the other direction.

He consulted with his patient in Tagalog and then, snuffing out his cigarette, motioned for the older man to approach the table.

"Seesters, stand beside me and watch everything that I do," he instructed. "He has a swollen hip and I will remove the infection."

I carefully helped the old man onto the table and watched Tony go through the motions that had now become so familiar to me. He placed his hands on the man's hip, closed his eyes to pray for a moment, and then I heard the popping sound of the flesh giving way under the tremendous pressure that emitted from his hands. Tony squeezed the infected liquid from a cotton ball and then allowed the aperture to close. With a quick wipe of the cotton, the skin on the hip was clean, the swelling already reduced by about half. The man got up, blessed all of us, and left with the boy, promising to return next week. It occurred to me that I would be gone by then and I felt sad.

The morning progressed, filled with patients with many different ailments. They complained of bad teeth, goiters on the neck, headaches, and hemorrhoids, but there wasn't a bad stomach in the lot. As the people arrived and spoke with Tony about their ailments, I waited to see if this might be my patient. When I learned that they had something that I could not work on, I first felt disappointment and then relief. Eventually, when I found myself praying for someone to have stomach problems, I knew that I had really gone off the deep end. At about eleven-thirty a large group of healthy stomachs left and I slumped back into my seat, starting to lose hope. Perhaps I would not get my chance. It was nearly lunchtime and it was doubtful that anyone else would be arriving. But I was not meant to miss my moment. The door downstairs squeaked open, banged shut, and up the stairs came a slightly overweight, middle-aged woman. She and Tony conversed in Tagalog and then Tony motioned for her to get on the table.

He turned to look at me and probed me with his piercing eyes. "It is her liver. You will do this one. Come up and stand here with me. We will pray."

I dartingly glanced at Lois, who gave me a promising nod. On quivering legs, I walked to the front of the room and took my place beside Tony as I had done so many times that week. But this time it was different. I flashed back to Bologna, Italy, when I was seventeen and about to perform my first solo role with the Harkness Ballet. As I heard Tony begin his prayers, I felt the ceremonial tap of knees on my derriere, the superstitious good-luck gesture bestowed by my fellow dancers in the wings of the theater. The heat and sunlight, which poured into the healing room, merged with the heat and brightness of the foot-lights beckoning me onto the stage. I had rehearsed many times in the safety of the rest of the company but even though I had full support from my friends and teachers, I would be out on stage, completely on my own. Tony was here to guide me in this present experience, but it was all up to me.

He motioned for me to place my hand on the woman's stomach and I saw the stage manager signal to me that the curtain was opening. As my hand touched the woman's flesh, I felt the sureness of the floor beneath my feet as I took my first step alone out onto the stage. The feelings poured over and through me. The need of the woman for healing. The rush of the audience, straining their energies toward me. Loss of in-nocence. Total vulnerability. Complete exposure to the un-known. Risk! The suggestion of the possibility of failure. The emergence of a part of me that only knew success.

My fingers began to probe around looking for the sign of the spot through which to enter. I thought I had it and began to press my fingers in. They hit the barrier. The footlights were shining in my eyes and I couldn't see. I pushed harder and harder. Nothing happened. I couldn't get through. I couldn't hear the music. I was out of touch. I began to panic. Tony touched me gently and moved my hands an inch to the left.

"Move your fingers around like you have seen me do," he instructed.

I breathed deeply and while my fingers perfectly mimicked the motion of that of my teacher, the music poured through in SenSurround. I was no longer blinded and I could feel my center. I continued my dance, intuitively knowing exactly what to do, and in another moment, I watched blood seeping up through my fingers.

I was strongly aware of Tony's presence, and with each movement that I made, I was in touch with the support and approval of my choreographer watching my progress from the wings. But I was almost numb. Although I was sure that something was happening, I was disconnected from my physical sensations. Even though I was doing it, somehow I was missing it.

I couldn't feel my hands inside her flesh, but I continued the action until it was finished. I tossed away the blood clot that appeared on the cotton ball I was holding and, when I removed my hands from the woman's body, I walked offstage.

I could hear the applause like a distant thundering in my head, and my first feeling was that of relief. Then, elation, and finally, depression. All that I had done wrong began to torment me and, because I had lost contact with the feeling in my hands, I doubted that I had healed her. Suddenly, I no longer knew if I had really done anything at all. I had thought it would be different. Maybe Tony had tricked me into making me believe that I had done something. Now I was sure that he had made the blood appear. I looked at him accusingly as all the color drained from my cheeks. I felt exhausted and angry. I knew that he could read my frustration.

He stared directly into my eyes and began to laugh. Teresa, who had been sitting at the back of the room, also burst into hysterics. I looked from one to the other, feeling furious and embarrassed.

I pulled him to the side of the room, away from the woman who was still lying on the table.

"Who did that? Was it me or you?" I demanded to know.

"You were in trance. You don't know what happened. That's why you could not feel anything," he informed me between his giggling bursts. "You can't remember but your energy was strong enough to magnetize the tissue and bring it through to the cotton in your hand. You sit down now while I give Lois a chance to *fractice*."

Now I was really confused. I walked to the bench, completely spent. I fell into my seat, and stared at the permanent indentations that the tight pointe shoe ribbons had left on my ankles. I closed my eyes and I could see myself after the performance, sitting alone in that Italian dressing room, studying my face in the mirror. The sweat was pouring off me as it always did after a long performance and I took a tissue from my purse and wiped my forehead while Lois and Tony completed their work on the woman. I didn't see what Lois did because I was too upset and confused to even watch.

By the time I had pulled myself together, the woman was getting off the table. She graciously thanked Lois and Tony and then walked over to me. She put her hand on my head, blessed me for helping her, and dropped a small donation into the box. I felt helpless, knowing that I had done nothing. Or had I? I just wasn't sure. This wasn't the way I had imagined it. I had done my first operation and I was now supposed to be elated and feeling special. Where was that feeling of power, of accomplishment? I was only upset and confused. Was this the way I had felt in Italy after that performance? I couldn't remember and I didn't even care anymore.

I looked over at Lois, wondering if she shared my confusion and despair. But as usual, she appeared to be quite peaceful. Her constant state of contentment and acceptance was beginning to irritate me. A wave of loneliness hit me and I wanted to go home where you could count on things, where doctors wore white coats and matter was matter.

After the woman left, Teresa scurried into the kitchen to put food on the table. Lois and I exchanged glances and she smiled at me reassuringly. Tony smoked a cigarette and I stared out the window. We said nothing to each other. He was letting me cool down. I nibbled at my lunch to be polite, eating very little and tasting nothing. When we were finished eating, Tony spoke to me.

"You must go back to your room and rest. You must *fray* to the Holy Spirit to help you in your healing work. You both brought up some blood and helped that woman. Now you must *fractice* in your home. Even though you will be leaving for Los Angeles very soon, I will continue to *fray* for you and I will help you even when you are not here. I can do this. I know how to travel in the astral and visit you in your home. The Holy Spirit has told me that you are both healers."

He pulled me close to him and hugged me. I hugged him back, tears of sadness and frustration filling my eyes. My insides felt torn by my desire to remain longer with him and by my need to go home and return to some semblance of life as I knew it. We walked down to the street, and I wondered if I would ever see Tony again. We hailed a taxi, climbed inside and melted into the back seat. And we were a yellow streak of speed, feeding into the continuous body of motion that filled the Manila streets.

I opened the windows wide, inviting the outside world to overwhelm my senses. We sped by splashes of color and harsh sounds, and I let the tears flow. Lois reached out her hand and I took it, but I could not be comforted. I inhaled the funky street smells of fried bananas, diesel fumes, and broken sewage pipes. I no longer recoiled from them. They were just Manila and I knew I would miss them.

The taxi stopped at a red light and we were hounded by merchants who ran out into the street to try to sell us their newspapers, cigarettes, and sweets. Feeling invaded, I shook my head at them and they backed off, running on to the next car. A beggar with a crippled leg slowly made his way through the traffic and shoved his dirty hand in the window, pleading with us to give him some money. Feeling his pain, I reached into my pocket. I wondered how he had hurt his leg and if he knew that he was in the land of healers. Perhaps it was not necessary for him to be crippled. Perhaps he had the ability to heal himself, but he either didn't believe it or didn't know it. I handed him a few coins which he greedily grabbed and he limped away before the cars started up again.

My mind flashed pictures of some of the incredible people I had met in the last few weeks. Although they looked somewhat like me, spoke a version of my language, and shared the same emotions, there was something different about them. It was their potency. It was the way their minds worked in harmony with their desires. These people believed in themselves and in their ability to heal. They were, each one of them, a powerful demonstration of human potential in action. It seemed that up until now, most of the people that I had come in contact with did not truly believe in themselves, or anyone else, for that matter.

I thought of my own life, especially of my childhood desire to lay hands on people. Although my mind had never been able to grasp it, I had had an instinctual knowing about my personal healing abilities. Here in the Philippines was the first time that that potential had been recognized and supported. How could I go back to the United States knowing that there were no teachers for me to study with? I was leaving too soon. How could I possibly stop now? But I also yearned to go home where life was familiar and secure. I felt split and torn apart inside.

I was dreadfully upset when the taxi finally dropped us at the hotel. Feeling exhausted and confused, I dropped onto my bed and fell asleep with my clothes on.

14

THE
LABYRINTH

The sun is setting, balancing on the tip of the mountains like an unbroken egg yolk, casting formidable giant-like shadows on the land. I am feeling dwarfed, standing at the foot of one of these mountains, tracing strange and unfamiliar symbols in the brown earth with my feet. I see the elongated shadow of a man, and I look up to find Alex directly in front of me.

Beneath the small ray of sun that still lights up the earth, we sit on the ground facing each other. The symbols that I have drawn are between us. I feel the heat of the sun on my body and I watch Alex, who sits unmoving. Then, he reaches his hand, fingers first, into the earth and removes a handful of dirt, throwing it off to the side. He says nothing but I intuit that he wants me to do the same. I try to reach in, but I cannot penetrate the dirt floor. I exert a great deal of effort and finally break through, removing a small amount of dirt. I throw it off in the same direction. Alex sits like a sphinx, staring straight through me. Without breaking eye contact, he reaches back into the earth, more deeply this time, and removes an even larger handful of dirt. He throws it off and waits. It is my turn again. I breathe deeply, place my hand on the earth and suddenly, I feel it open easily and smoothly. I reach in effortlessly and remove a large handful of dirt and throw it away. I feel elated. It was so easy. We do this process several more times.

Alex leans forward and says to me, "I can teach you to do what I do." Adrenalin rushes through my body. I hardly dare to think that this could be true. I try to engage him in further conversation. Even though his words were clear, I feel that I have misunderstood him.

"Do you mean that you can teach me to operate like you do?" I ask. He says nothing. I plead with him to answer me but he remains silent. His physical presence begins to dissolve and I am left with a yearning feeling. The sun drops behind the mountains with a loud buzzing sound, jolting my entire nervous system.

I awakened with a start, and bolted out of bed. I was in a cold sweat and I was shaking. Lois's bed was empty and I remembered she had gone to spend the night with her friend Chuchi. I must have been in a very deep sleep when she left. My clothes stuck to my body as I peeled them off, dropping them to the floor at my feet. Glad that I was alone, I walked into the bathroom and turned on the shower, shivering while I waited for the water to heat up.

As the hot water splashed over me, I sighed deeply, hoping that the wet heat would eradicate some of my uncomfortable feelings. There had been something unnerving in that dream. The first thing that I had noticed when I met Alex was the love that flowed from him. In the dream, it was absent, replaced by a coolness that I had never seen in him. He had appeared almost zombie-like. There was something vital that was missing from his being, some attitude of rigidity that he was reflecting to me. When he said that he could teach me to do what he did, somehow

I knew that he wasn't talking about surgery. But what was he talking about? I hadn't the faintest idea.

I stepped out of the shower and dried myself off. Pulling on a soft cotton T-shirt, I looked at the time. It was three o'clock in the morning and I felt terrible. I paced back and forth, unable to quiet my nerves. My mind was racing, flashing disconnected pictures of caves, waterfalls, blood, sick people, and distorted spirit forms. I looked out the window, trying to control my mind by concentrating on the ever-changing colors of the Las Vegas–style fountain in front of the hotel. Red to yellow to green to blue to purple to white and on and on to infinity. But rather than having a calming effect, these artificial colors disturbed me and I pulled myself away from the light show, feeling as if something had been attempting to brainwash me.

I tried to sit down and cool my mind, but the heat was rising steadily. I began to pace back and forth again, Alex's words haunting me. *I can teach you to do what I do. I can teach you to do what I do.* What did it mean? Why was I suddenly awakened in the middle of the night? Was this some kind of sign? Was my destiny being decided for me? Why didn't it feel joyful? Why was I upset and confused? What had really happened at Tony's? I felt lightheaded and I poured myself a glass of water. I drank thirstily and sat at the edge of the bed, folded my hands in my lap, and tried to regulate my breathing. It was time to think this thing out rationally.

I was torn and unhappy, knowing that the day after tomorrow, I would be leaving for home. But I was afraid to go home. I had found magic in this faraway land and had come so close to breaking through to another level. I dreaded returning to my mundane existence of ordinary people, occupations and experiences. I wanted to be a healer. How could I ever want anything else after what I had done over these last few weeks? But how could I achieve what I wanted, back in the United States, where nobody even believed these things existed? I had just had a dream that was trying to tell me something. Perhaps it was letting me know that I was destined for greatness, something beyond the humdrum life that was available to the rest of the world. I just needed more time. I noticed that I was pacing again.

I had always hoped that I could do something that would single me out from all the others. Perhaps this was it. Tony said that the Spirit told him that I was a healer. I really wanted to heal people. I wanted them to feel about me the way I felt about Alex, Camilo, and Tony. I wanted to be someone who could take people out of their misery. If I could just learn to do this, how could I ever feel anything but wonderful? How could anything else ever be important enough to trouble me? My dream, even though it had seemed strange, could have been letting me know that Alex thought I was special enough to be like him. That must have been what it meant. The thoughts churned round and round in my head.

Maybe I should just disappear from my regular world and make a commitment to studying healing with Alex and Tony. But I was afraid to stay. What if I stayed and gave up everything that meant anything to me and I ended up not being able to do psychic surgery? Then I would be worse off than before. What was I supposed to do? I needed help but whom could I talk to? Who would understand? I felt isolated and desperate.

My thoughts raced as if I were chasing after something. I felt as if my mind were a labyrinth and I were rushing down the corridors looking for a way out. At every turn, I saw doors with green neon exit signs promising deliverance from all that I was repelled by. But when I got to the door, the neon turned red and the people that I loved the most were standing beneath the exit signs. I would have to face them to pass through the door, but I just couldn't. What I was most repelled by was my own attitude, and I didn't want them to see me like this. There must be another way that I could sneak out without being exposed. I caught sight of a new corridor that I hadn't noticed before. It looked like a clear escape. The exit sign seductively flashed in green with no one standing beneath it. I started to run for it. Just a few more steps and I would be at the door. As I reached for the doorknob, I froze.

The door had become a huge distorted mirror and there I was, staring into my own twisted face. I gazed with horror at this image of myself, my crooked head twice as large as my body. Something inside of me screamed out, "You can only be yourself and that will never change." I turned to run but I could not. Behind me stood yet another mirror. I was trapped by my own reflection and I had no choice but to face it. I stood gaping at the distorted form I had become and I sobbed in agony. As I forced myself to see what I was projecting, the mirror images slowly dissolved and I found myself standing on the floor of my room at the hotel.

Exhausted, I threw myself down on the bed and covered my eyes with my arm, blocking out the light. As the tears poured out, Boy's gentle smiling face appeared in front of me. As soon as I saw him, I let go. I dropped my arm from my face and allowed my body to relax. I would talk to him. I knew he could help me figure things out. But I didn't have his phone number. A wave of panic washed over me once again.

I jumped up. Jimmy! He would have Boy's number. I grabbed for the telephone and then realized it was four o'clock in the morning. I didn't think Jimmy would appreciate my call. I would have to wait. I knew that once I talked to Boy, everything would be all right. I lay back down on the bed, hoping to catch some sleep. I was weary but I could not relax enough to go unconscious. I breathed, I conjured what I thought were calming images, I counted backwards, but nothing worked.

I got up and walked to the window, looking out over the sleepy streets of Manila. In the distance I could see the sparkling glow of small boats floating in Manila Bay. My eyes strayed back to the monotonous changing of the lights in the hotel fountain. There my brain was temporarily anesthetized as I watched the colors switch from one to the next, on through the night, until the sun began to peek out onto the horizon. I was rescued from my hypnosis as the artificial colors disappeared, replaced by a beautiful natural sunrise coming up over the water.

As I turned my face to the rainbow rays of light and allowed them to heal me, I was released from my labyrinth of despair. I gratefully climbed between the cool sheets and slept a dreamless sleep, comforted by the nurturing light of day.

15

CENTERING

I awakened when Lois returned from Chuchi's. It was about noon and I was groggy and depressed. She tried to cheer me up and pull me out of my mood by inviting me to go shopping, but I wasn't interested. She could see I didn't really want to talk, so she left and I spent the afternoon in seclusion, thinking, dozing, and staring at the walls. I reached Jimmy, who gave me two home numbers for Boy, but I could not get through. One number was continuously busy and the other was temporarily out of order. When I finally got the first one to ring, there was nobody home. I tried for several hours and then I gave up.

Lois came back laden with gifts for her friends back home. She made me get up and have a snack with her, but I could hardly eat. I returned back to the room and we both took a nap. At about five the phone rang. I rushed to pick it up. It was Jimmy.

"Have you spoken with Boy?" he asked.

"No," I answered. "I can't get through. I feel so frustrated."

"Welcome to the Manila phone dilemma, the most inefficient communication system in the world. Now you can understand firsthand why we are all so psychic. It is out of necessity."

I smiled for the first time since the day before.

"You sound depressed. Is there anything I can do for you?" he asked.

"I don't think so. I just need to think."

"Better not do too much of that. It might get you in trouble. I called to remind you that Chuchi de Vega is having a big party tonight. She wants to wish you and Lois a special farewell since you are departing tomorrow."

I moaned. Attending a party was the last thing in the world that I felt like doing. "I don't know, Jimmy. I didn't sleep very well last night and I don't think I'm up to it."

"What are you going to do? Just sit in your room and mope? I'll pick you both up at seven-thirty."

I didn't have the energy to protest.

"All right, but I can't guarantee what mood I'll be in."

"Just relax. Things have a way of taking care of themselves. I'll see you in a few hours."

I hung up the phone and tried to reach Boy again. I still didn't know exactly why, but I had to speak with him. Both lines were still blocked. Then I remembered Jimmy's words about psychic communication. It was certainly worth a try. Nothing else had worked. I lay down on my bed, closed my eyes, and pictured Boy in as much detail as I could. I saw his twinkling brown eyes, his round boyish face, and his perpetual Buddha-like smile. I called out to him and told him that I needed to see him, to talk to him. I asked him to please hear me and to respond. Satisfied that I had done everything I could, I meditated and relaxed for a while.

At about seven Lois began to get ready for the party. She came out of the bathroom, opened the closet and threw a dress at me. "Come on. Just forget about it and get ready. This is our last night in Manila, and Chuchi is really going out of her way to do something nice for us. It'll be good to get out and take your mind off yourself for a while. You might even have a good time. Stranger things have happened in the Philippines."

I managed a good-natured laugh, went into the bathroom, and splashed some cold water on my face. I reluctantly got dressed, gazing at the telephone with anxiety. Boy and I had still not connected and I wondered if I should try to reach him again. But then Jimmy called to tell us that he was waiting in the lobby. I grabbed my purse, resigned myself to a long, boring evening, and we headed for the elevator.

Chuchi de Vega lived about thirty minutes from the hotel in a beautiful section of town. Jimmy knew that I was uncomfortable, so he let me be with my thoughts; he and Lois chatted as we drove. We entered through the security gate and pulled up in front of Chuchi's lushly furnished palatial home, filled to the brim with guests from all over the world. Chuchi came running out to greet us. She hugged us warmly.

"Hello! Hello! I'm so happy to see you. Please come in and meet everybody."

We walked in on a typical bustling party scene with maids running back and forth offering drinks and hors d'oeuvres. People were milling around, sharing toasts and discussing the latest developments in the ever-volatile Philippine political situation. Jimmy went to greet some close friends and I wandered away, feeling very withdrawn and out of place in this wilderness of strange faces.

I wandered from room to room, taking in the vastness and the beauty of Chuchi's elaborate home. Each room was tastefully decorated with antiques, finely crafted Philippine wood carvings, hand-painted ceilings, and marbled floors. The grounds were manicured to perfection, and I admired her collection of miniature bonsai plants and exotic birds. She loved animals and nature and she had fashioned her home around her passions.

I spoke with a few people but I really had no interest in them. I tried to make myself invisible as I floated around the house, looking for a quiet spot where no one would engage me in conversation. I found a loveseat in a corner that was partially hidden by the immense leaves of a giant tropical plant. I sat down, feeling safe from outside interference, and retreated into my inner world.

As far as I could tell, there was no good reason why I was at this party. But there was no good reason to be anywhere else, either, so I occupied myself by secretly watching people. Children were screaming and chasing each other around the room. Men and women were laughing and shyly flirting. I saw several young girls chatting and giggling and I recognized Chuchi's daughter, Maggie, as one of them. They looked so young and carefree, animatedly conversing in half English and half Tagalog. I envied them because they seemed so innocent. I wondered if I would ever feel lighthearted again. I felt as if I were trapped inside a web of confusion and depression. The sound of babbling voices and the clashing of random colors blended into one sound and one color that I found loud and irritating. I felt isolated and foreign, as if I didn't really belong here anymore. But as I searched my memory, it seemed that I didn't really belong back home either. I was a lost soul, an alien, and I fell into a sense of futility and self-pity. I had no desire to move and so there I sat, unnoticed and undisturbed, for what seemed like hours, with no interest or motivation.

"I guess you must be seeing so many things right now." I turned to see who was trying to intrude on my solitary misery and there stood Boy, in the flesh, smiling and twinkling at me. I jumped up and threw my arms around him.

"I have been trying to reach you. I didn't want to leave without seeing you first and I didn't know how to find you."

"I hope you didn't try the telephone," he kidded me. "Manila is not known for its efficiency in these areas."

He looked into my face, studying my eyes and he said, "Let's sit for a few minutes."

I had no idea how he had found me and I didn't bother asking him.

We sat down in my private corner and he turned to me and said, "You have seen so many things and now I want to tell you that there is only one thing that you have to do to be a healer. You must center yourself. That is all. It is so very simple." He threw back his head and laughed.

His laughter reverberated inside my stomach and I felt the tight muscles of my solar plexus begin to respond to the sound of his voice. How did he know what I needed to hear? Could he read my mind? I felt embarrassed that he might be able to read the insane turmoil that I was caught up in. What must he think of me? I hated to have him see me so unbalanced but it didn't really matter. He never seemed to mind. He just always knew exactly what to say to bring me back to myself.

"I feel confused," I said. "I don't know what is happening to me but nothing feels right. I am out of touch with myself."

"Let's go outside. There is too much psychic interference in here. We can walk and talk for a while."

He led me out into the balmy night. The air was humid and full, and the stars speckled the moonless sky like a burst of shimmering crystals. I piled my hair on top of my head to allow the tropical breezes to caress my neck.

We walked in silence for a few minutes and I imagined we were back at Mount Banahaw, tuning in to the rhythmical vibrations emanating from the earth. I began to feel my center for the first time since I had awakened in that panic. The longer we walked, the easier it became to think and listen. The silence that had been previously drowned out by my inner turmoil was returning. My breath was slowing down and I became aware that Boy and I were breathing in unison. The steady rhythm of our breathing was bringing my nervous system back into a state of calm.

Boy stopped, sat down on the earth, and motioned for me to sit beside him. He began to speak and I listened to his words, which were reaching me across the swaying tropical winds.

"This may sound strange to you, but in truth, healing is nothing more than meditation. Normally, people define meditation as a technique whereby one sits and tries to do or not do various things with the mind. But a technique requires effort. Meditation is non-effort. It simply happens. When I say that I am in meditation, I am merely saying that for that moment, I am in my totality. I am in my totality now as I talk. I am totally talking, therefore I am in meditation. My mind is rooted into what I am doing *now*. I am neither relating to the past nor projecting into the future.

"When I am in this state of totality, it is irrelevant what I am doing. What is important is that I have not separated myself. I am connected to the whole. I am not goal-oriented. I am spontaneous and that spontaneity is coming through my unconscious mind. By being totally at one with everything, I have opened up the gap between the conscious and the unconscious mind. I am functioning in a state I call the superconscious and now all minds are flowing into one. I am like a drop of water merging with the ocean. When I am in a meditative state of totality, I am no longer functioning as a drop. I am functioning as the entire ocean.

"Once in this state, all that the healer needs to do is to allow, and create situations for the patient to be at ease. The patient cannot be at peace with a plugged-up mind. As a healer, it is my effortless work to open myself enough to become a hollow conduit. Through this conduit, the perfect balance of the universe will naturally flow from me to the patient, allowing both of us to share a perfect state of ease and attunement. The only way that I can become centered enough to reach this state is by learning more and more about myself. It is through awareness that this state of totality becomes possible."

He studied my face. I felt his complete presence and I met him with my own. I knew that what he was saying was fundamentally important to me and I listened to him with all my attention.

"The moment I say that I healed you, I am lying. I am not the one who did it. Of course, I assisted you by becoming a clear enough channel for the energy to pass through. But you are the only one who can center and balance your own body and mind. All I can do is to employ a few simple techniques which provoke you to help yourself.

"For the healer, the basis of everything is the breath. When I take a moment to become aware of another's breathing patterns, I actually move into the vibratory layer of the patient. I become receptive. I feel what you are feeling and I become one with you. I can now penetrate to the subconscious layer and give telepathic messages that can help to unplug your mind so that centering can be achieved. This is the technique that I just used with you while we were walking. At first, you were all plugged up, but you responded to my suggestions and balanced yourself. I did not do it.

"I would not say that I can teach this technique to anyone. I learned it through my great desire to know more about myself and to increase my sensitivity. Once we learn to know our own bodies and minds, only then do we have the ability to become sensitive to others. This is what you did in Jacob's Well. By facing parts of you that you had previously hidden away, you were actually increasing your ability to know yourself and, therefore, to be able to heal. Healing is a personal search, a personal awakening. We are learning to heal for ourselves, not for others. If we are focusing on something outside ourselves, we are in separation and we are only serving our own egos. It is a sad thing that so many healers are lured into this ego trap. But the ego always provides us with a perfect opportunity to eventually confront this part of ourselves and move out of it. And so in this way, even the ego serves us."

Boy became silent for a moment, closed his eyes, and breathed. I did the same and became aware of our perfect alignment with all of the elements. He was able to show this to me, even here in the center of the city.

"In my earlier stages of healing, I was caught in an ego trap. I had a few techniques within my grasp and I walked around with a holier-than-thou attitude. I justified myself by saying that

I was serving humanity. I was functioning from my logical mind, not my heart. One day, I became aware that I was not enjoying my healing work. I was tired all the time and after healing sessions, I often became sick. My sickness forced me to stop and I began to observe myself. For the first time, I had to find out what healing was really about so that I could heal myself. I found that true service is spontaneous, an outpouring of love from a heart that is full. It is a natural by-product of becoming a healthy, balanced individual. Through my self-seeking, I noticed that when I became emotional and goal-oriented about service and my healing work, I was susceptible to picking up the patient's ailments. When I acquired an effortless attitude, I was in no danger. Perhaps I am still working out a few things with my ego, but I am aware of this and I am having a good time."

He smiled broadly. At that moment I understood why I felt so drawn to him. He really knew who he was and he liked and accepted himself. This was why I had needed to see him so badly. I needed a reflection of someone who was centered in his own reality so that I could see how to bring myself back in balance.

I spoke to him about my turmoil concerning my work with Tony and my obsessive desire to continue. He thought for a while and then he spoke.

"When a person does psychic surgery spontaneously, it is good. It comes because God intended for it to be so. This is how many of the healers do their work and they stay healthy and strong and help many people. But when it does not come naturally and we begin to try to manipulate ourselves, we are going against our own true nature. Then we have problems."

He smiled knowingly and I wondered what he was leading up to.

"Did you know that I was very sick a few years ago because of this very problem? Can you imagine, Andrea, that I had muscular dystrophy?"

I couldn't believe it. I had seen him skillfully crawling around the rocks on Mount Banahaw. He certainly did not look like someone who had a crippling muscular disease.

"Yes, it's true," he said, beaming with joy. "I used to study magic. I learned to create healing by mantras and manipulation. It was a secret system that did not empower the patient. It was like a game to me and I did it for my ego. You see, if you meditate and chant, you may naturally and organically go into the higher vibrational frequencies. If it is a natural phenomenon for you to astral travel, it is no strain. But if you try to induce yourself to go into astral traveling, you have to force yourself to violently fluctuate from the lower to the higher frequencies. This is what I did. These frequencies are so opposite, I became biologically all mixed up. After several years of playing a very dangerous game, it affected my nervous system. That is to say, my nervous system just cramped up.

"Every three or four months, I kept having cramp attacks during which I couldn't breathe or move. Finally, I could no longer walk. A family member suggested that I was being possessed by evil spirits and maybe one of my healer friends could help me. But I knew better, because I, myself, was doing exorcisms. So I got in touch with an *herbularia,* a natural healer. She examined me and told me that I had blockages in the meridians of the nerve points. She said that the unnatural games that I was playing with magic had hurt me biologically and the nerves in my muscles were all clogged up. I knew that she was right.

"I had already been forced to stop my outside healing work. Now I had to heal myself. She told me to get into a bath with herbs and she did massage on my muscles every other day. She used to tell me, 'Boy, you have a certain talent. Why are you not using it?' I listened but I didn't know what she meant. In a period of four weeks, I could walk."

"When did you resume your healing work again?" I asked him.

"It was many months later when I was back at work. An

office mate sprained his leg and I began spontaneously to massage him because I cared about him. He improved quickly. Then I knew what talent my healer friend was talking about. After that, things changed. I went back into healing out of gratitude, with a true commitment to use it as a vehicle to learn about myself."

I had never imagined that Boy had gone through such a shattering experience. I felt so grateful that he trusted me enough to expose these personal things to me. I could see our parallels in my obsession with the magical lure of psychic surgery. I had forgotten my own truth while I was trying to force myself to do something that would win people's attention. I asked him if he had ever wanted or tried to do psychic surgery.

"Because I grew up in the Philippines," Boy said, "psychic surgery was all around me and did not seem so extraordinary. I was never heavily drawn to the phenomenon because I could find nothing of myself in it. It is important to examine the reasons that we are attracted to certain realities. Being healed by a phenomenon is exciting, but what does it do for one's personal awareness? Since we know self-healing is the only way to achieve balance, we must find a way to empower others to know themselves better. We must get to the root cause of the illness and suggest a way that individuals may become centered and balanced in their own realities and learn to find their own healing center within. Merely removing the symptoms by means of a phenomenon will do nothing for an individual's consciousness. They will soon recreate the illness because the centering was never achieved.

"I think, Andrea, that healers in the West have a better opportunity to develop their own inherent abilities through their healing practice. Because there are no shortcuts, they must proceed at a pace equal to their personal evolution. Here in the Philippines, many of us have the tendency to turn to spirit intervention because it is so readily available and we know how to do such things. A young healer can appear very powerful almost immediately with the cooperation of a spirit, but what is that healer doing for himself? The power is only serving the ego because there is no challenge to stretch to the next level of personal development. Don't you agree?

"It is the natural evolution of a human being to evolve spiritually. When a healer truly maintains focus on spiritual development, both personally and for the patient, the results can be long lasting. Then the healer is flowing with nature. It is against nature to turn from attraction, so if you are heavily drawn to the psychic surgery phenomenon, follow it because you must. There is teaching in it for you. Just remember to stay aware of what you are doing and why. Then you are in no danger."

His voice was like a soothing melody. He reached into his pocket, pulled something out, and handed it to me. "I have a gift for you. This is a piece of 'dignum' wood that can only be found on the peaks of Mount Banahaw. There are three different types of this wood. The next time I see you, I will give you the second variety. I have carved a yin-yang symbol into this one, the representation of the perfect male-female balance of life. I left two open holes where you could place crystals. Perhaps it will serve as a reminder to you."

I folded my fingers over it, vowing to always remember these things that he had told me. Tears came to my eyes and I knew that we were saying good-bye. He hugged me and began to walk back into the house. He suddenly turned his eternal smile to face me one last time and said, "You have only to be who you are. What could be more perfect or special than expressing what nature has intended for you to be?"

I watched him walk away while I cried softly. I needed to be alone to think so I crossed the street and headed toward an open field surrounding an old cathedral. As the wind made the trees dance, I could see how everything moved and changed continuously: the air, the trees, and my feelings about myself. I sat beneath a huge palm tree, and felt the coolness of the wind drying my tears on their pathway down my face. I tasted the saltiness as the new ones flowed down the tear-trails on my cheeks and into my mouth. My senses were alert and I was totally aware of my connection with the fertility and aliveness of nature. I knew that I had the ability to create and nourish anything that I chose. But what did I really want for myself? Perhaps I didn't know yet.

I thought about Boy and Waway and my deep love and admiration for them. They were among the most special people that I had ever met. Their specialness had come through to me in the form of who they are, what they naturally expressed from the depths of their beings. It was their relationship with themselves that made them so attractive to me. They seemed to be more aware and in touch with themselves than anyone else that I had ever met. I could see their powerful healing potency because they had influenced me greatly in my own process of self-awareness. They had provoked me into facing my fears and hidden emotions. They had allowed me to confront my blocks and to become acquainted with a courage I never knew I had. They had taught me to laugh at myself and to suspend self-judgment so that I could learn from my actions.

Boy and Waway had led me along a journey back to center, one which had automatically awakened and activated the truth that lives within me. And they had never tried to teach me anything. They did it all by maintaining their own personal centers and demonstrating a state of balance and self-love. I knew they were true healers because they had given me the greatest gift possible: more of myself. They had shown me my personal connection to the natural flow of all that is, the most special attribute that can be attained.

Alex's face floated into my mind. And I now understood the message of the dream. His coolness was merely a reflection of my own, my disconnection from my heart. When he said that he could teach me to do what he does, he was not necessarily referring to psychic surgery. He was speaking about his ability to concentrate totally on whatever he is doing at the time. He was referring to his total involvement in expressing exactly who he is at each moment.

I remembered the story that Lois told me about Alex's life.

When he was young, he had tried to run away from who he was, but he almost died. He had learned the hard way. He saw that I wanted to be like him and he was trying to tell me to be who I am. Everybody I had met and respected was giving me the same message. I laughed out loud when I realized what extremes it took to get me to listen.

One of the teachings of Mount Banahaw was about experiencing all sides of one's being before a spiritual choice could be made. So this was what my trip was about. I was here in the Philippines to go deeper within myself so that I might awaken to my own truth. And I found that there was a wealth of untapped resources and creativity inside of me, just waiting to be given the chance to express themselves. I could now focus on myself in ways that I would no longer label selfish. The real Andrea had been living dormant within me and was being born anew at this moment.

Lois had been the greatest teacher of them all by not trying to push or change me. She had been with me every day, watched my whole dance, the ego trips, the obsessive behavior, the pain and sorrow, and she had let me go through it all in my own time. She had simply maintained her own center and her own light. What a lesson in friendship. I was so glad I didn't have to leave her behind.

The thought of going back home now filled me with excitement and anticipation. Living in harmony with nature, I could have whatever I wanted, anywhere that I was. I could hardly wait to see my friends. I felt that as I opened more of myself to them, they would naturally show me more of who they were. Now it seemed that all my relationships were superficial compared with what I knew I could have.

I stood up and allowed the fluttering winds to blow through me, making me a hollow conduit for the universe to fill up. If physical healing turned out to be my future expression, then I would certainly allow it. If not, I knew that whatever I chose would be a form of healing if I utilized it to express myself, my individuality, my connectedness with the world. I was ready to return to the party, to interact with and appreciate myself and everyone else. The wind playfully rippled my clothing as I ran across the street, anxious to see my friends who were having a party.

As I opened the door, the sound of laughter washed over me, filling me with joy. I felt like I had come home. Jimmy came running over to greet me.

"You look so different. That walk in the fresh air did you a world of good," he said approvingly.

"Oh Jimmy, you have no idea."

We walked around the party together and he introduced me to some of his friends. We found Lois and when she looked at me, she knew something had changed. She asked no questions and the three of us spent the remainder of the evening together. We went from group to group, laughing and having a wonderful time. It seemed impossible that these were the same people I had been hiding from. Each one was unique and wonderful and I could connect with everyone because I was centered in myself. I felt strong and beautiful, like a radiant beam of light. I did not see Boy again that night but I felt him smiling inside me as I knew he always would.

Jimmy drove us to the airport the next day. I was ready to go back home, but I was sad to leave these people I loved. Only passengers were allowed beyond the front door leading into the terminal building. Jimmy and I embraced at the door, and when he walked away, I knew that, just as we had returned to Mount Banahaw, someday we would be back together again.

The plane had barely left Philippine shores, and I could already feel the separation tugging on my solar plexus. I drifted through the magnificent cloud formations, giving thanks that I had awakened enough to be able to feel this much. And I flew back home.

16

INTEGRATION

I walked down the stairs from the plane feeling like a time traveler disembarking into a past life. A dry wind scratched at my face, and the Los Angeles airport looked sterile and high-tech. Everything felt overly large and imposing, like a legendary giant I had known well but had not seen for some time.

Customs was a swift process and I was greatly relieved to be back in America where efficiency reigned. I was tired and wanted to go home. Cleared by a bored-looking customs agent, I walked through the revolving door which spun me into the lobby of the Los Angeles International terminal. I was never so acutely aware of how far away I had been than at this moment of my return.

Lois and I hugged good-bye and went our separate ways; she took the limousine service back to the desert and I got into a taxi to go home. I watched the scenery flash by, feeling like a child who was seeing everything for the first time.

The next few weeks were about readjustment to time, to

places, to life. Each time I closed my eyes to meditate or to sleep, I was transported back to Mount Banahaw. I walked down the steps to Santa Lucia, I climbed the mountainsides, I soaked in the tranforming waters of Jacob's Well. While I was unwilling to give up this much-desired state of bilocation, I also found it disturbing. Most mornings I awoke groggy and disoriented, not really connecting to the world around me for several hours after rising. I was hardly seeing any people. I just wasn't ready yet. Although it felt right to be back home, I was resisting withdrawing from the magical reality that had so greatly affected me.

I awakened particularly exhausted one day and called Lois. I told her that I was tired and irritable and I didn't quite know what to do about it.

"It's time to come home, Andrea," she said. "It's not doing you any good to be in two places at once because you are not really present in either place. You have left a vital part of yourself behind and it's impossible to function properly. It's time to call your spirit back here again, which you have the power to do anytime you want. You won't be giving up anything. What you did and where you were will always be yours. Besides, you have work to do."

I knew she was right. It was time to be present and integrate what I had learned into my everyday existence. That night before I slept, I prayed. I gave thanks for the people I had met and the things I had learned. I asked for all of me to come back home. I spoke to my wandering spirit and commanded it back into my body. I pictured my many separate parts being pulled together by a magnetic force until they merged into one full person. I was ready to integrate all the new knowledge I had been given and really put it to use. All at once, an energy surged through me and I knew I had landed. I felt secure, whole, and filled with light. I slept peacefully that night and awoke happy and ready to face my world as a complete woman, with a great deal to share with people.

I spent wonderful evenings telling my friends stories about my adventures and they could hardly wait to come back to hear more. I was simply being myself and the response was fantastic. I reconnected with my friend Laurie, and it was such a joy to laugh with her again. We had really missed each other and our reunion filled a gap in my life. I began to develop the magnetic healing I had learned in the Philippines and people loved it. In a short time, I had a small practice and I was enjoying what I was doing. My luck had shifted and the difficulty I had been experiencing before my trip was over. I don't know whether it was the specific things I had learned or just a fresh energy inside of me, but everything I tried worked.

After I had been home for several weeks and my life was feeling good, I decided I wanted to pay Lois a visit. I wanted to share with her in person the changes that had happened to me and to ask her to teach me to do facials. It seemed like becoming a facialist would be a perfect vehicle both spiritually and financially. It would also be another way to stay connected to Lois. More than ever, I wanted to continue working with her. She was very receptive to the idea, so I headed out to the desert.

We spent a joyful weekend reminiscing and laughing about all of our adventures. We pored through hundreds of photographs, recalling places and people we both knew so well. I didn't know how to express to her the importance the trip had held for me, but it was unnecessary. She could see how much my life had changed.

We spoke about my dark days of confusion and my talk with Boy. She had known what I was going through but she also knew that it was my battle and that I would have to come through it on my own.

"Now you understand why I told you to remember who you are," she commented.

"Yes, I do, but I didn't at the time. It was something I had to learn for myself. How can I ever thank you enough for bringing me with you?"

"Don't thank me. Just be yourself and that's all the thanks I'll ever need." She really understood what it was to be real and to naturally empower all the people around her. She was a living example and a constant reminder.

We discussed at length the operations we had performed with Tony and the dilemma of still not knowing what really occurred. She didn't really know either. She could tell me only what she saw, that she saw both of us bring up blood and beyond that, she knew no more than I did.

On Sunday evening, as dusk approached, Lois was busy preparing her famous chicken soup, the cure-all that her Ukrainian mother had taught her to make. It was my favorite time of day so I walked up the hill to watch the sunset. It was blustery and dry, and the biting wind blew the sand into wild flurries. The cacti were lit up in phosphorescent green, and the tough and scratchy bushes were battling the harsh breezes. Nature was always so severe in the desert. When it was cold, everything froze. When it was hot, it burned. The winds were treacherous, the stillness could drive a person insane.

I stopped at the top of a small hill and chose a spot to sit and watch the sunset. I wrapped my arms around me for protection from the intrusive winds and watched the colors begin to appear on the horizon as the orange fireball started its lavish descent behind the mountains. Peaches and reds poured out from the sky and enveloped me in their reflections. I remembered another time in a faraway place when I bathed myself in the rainbows of an enchanted world. These same healing rays of light had been present to calm me in Manila when I could not stop my brain. It was thousands of miles away from here, but they were the same colors. It was the same light.

I dug my fingers into the dry, pebbly sand of the desert. It was different from the wet, fertile earth in the Philippines and yet, it was still the earth. The winds whipped around, dancing with the bushes and my fly-away hair. Although they felt cold here, they were the same winds that tickled the trees and blew through me in the open field across from Chuchi's house. Nature was expressing herself in similar ways everywhere in the world. She had been creating, healing, integrating, and disintegrating all life forms since the beginning of time. And I was an integral part of this natural process of creation and dissolution, of life and death.

I watched the cloud formations being brilliantly painted by the sun while highlights of my trip played through my mind. It was all alive inside of me, a bittersweet memory of a magnificent time that would never return. A deep sadness filled me as the faces of these loving people who had so greatly influenced my life appeared in my mind's eye. I looked at each one of them, heard them speak and tried to communicate with them, but all I could feel was separation. They were gone and I was alone. I cried aloud and the sounds of my sobs were stolen by the swirling desert gales. My emptiness felt magnified by the streaming colors of the sunset.

Shivering from the winds, I stood to leave, when I felt a strong and familiar presence around me. I turned to stare straight into the light of the sun and was entranced by glowing images which were starting to form in front of me, backlit by the magnificent Western skies. As they gradually took form, I saw vibrating light images of Boy, Waway, Jimmy, Alex, Camilo, David, and Tony with their arms outstretched toward me. Their eyes burned orange like the sun. Pouring out of their hands were radiant sparks of colored light. I stood perfectly still while they showered me with the healing light of nature. I allowed the colors to encircle and penetrate me while I basked in the glow of their love and warmth.

I opened my heart to take in this gift that was being bestowed upon me. This natural light was the healing power that existed within all of us and I was now awake enough to recognize it. I reached my hands out to them to complete the healing circle and saw the same colored sparks of radiance shoot out from my own fingertips, encircling them with my love. With orange light still glowing in my eyes, I turned to face the darkness of the eastern sky. I knew that I need not miss my friends because whenever I wanted them, I could find them vibrating within me. Without looking back, I ran down the hill toward the house.